YOU WERE MADE FOR THIS

A 91 DAY DEVOTIONAL FOR MILITARY SPOUSES

WRITTEN BY: KATHERINE MONIT

Cover design by Tracy Tyrrell

Affectionately dedicated to my amazing husband, Samuel, my prince, who has made my life a complete military adventure. I love you so much.

Acknowledgments

To my amazing parents; Garry and Cheryl Palmer. You both have shaped my life by being true examples of a follower of Jesus Christ and continually encouraging me to follow Gods plans for my life. I love you so much.

To my incredible in laws; Leo and Roseanne Monit. Thank you both for raising such a Godly man, and for loving me like your own. I love you both.

I wish to express special appreciation to my sweet children, Elijah, Michael and Adella. I love you three so much and I am so thankful for each of you!

To Audra Kennedy for her wholehearted dedication in editing. Your attention to detail has been a blessing. Thank you for helping me put my words in order to help reach more souls for Christ.

To Tracy Tyrrell for her beautiful cover design. She truly is a mom (of six) that does it all. I am thankful for you and your amazing gift.

To Naomi Koebbe, Jeni Castle and Kristyn Sandoval who have each blessed me with such a cherished friendship for over 25 years.

To Jill James for giving me a push to dream a new dream.

To all my military friends who have become sisters by military. I know that one day we will all be together again.

You Were Made For This

By Katherine Monit

Day 1

Strength

Jeremiah 16:19, "Lord, my strength and my fortress, my refuge in time of distress..."

You have God's strength. His grace is in you!

S-trive T-o R-each E-very N-ew G-rowth T-hru H-im

There are things in your life that are going to seem overwhelming at first, but God offers you His strength every day. When you say to Him, "Lord, I just can't do this today without you." He hears you and He gives you the strength and grace to do exactly what needs to be done. It's amazing. You will see doors opening that many have said, "There is no way that will happen for you." They may have even made remarks, "you're too slow, overweight, or labeled with a disorder, the list goes on. God, however, can turn the impossible into the possible because you used the strength He gave you.

During a women's conference at our church in California, I went to the altar, knelt down, and asked God to give me the strength I needed to be the best wife to Samuel and the best mom to my three children. As I was praying, one of the leaders came over and began praying with me. When we were through, she looked at me and said, "Katherine, God has given you the strength and grace to be the women He has called you to be. You have to give yourself grace, too. Don't put so much pressure on yourself that life seems unbearable." Wow. I've reminded myself of those words so many times when I was pushing too hard in my own strength.

Now, I'm saying the same thing to you today: Give yourself grace.

You are doing such a great job being you with all the different things you do each day (seriously all!). When you give yourself grace, you'll find yourself saying no to certain things in order to say yes to the things God has designed for you and the things that really need to be on the top of your priority list.

If you're already committed to a job, volunteering at the church, or being an awesome spouse, there will be things that come up to distract you. Be cautious of that. I enjoy doing more than one thing at a time; consequently, that can also turn into…burn out (and no one likes burnt chocolate!). I had to learn that truth along the way.

You're only one person! Yes, you have a lot of gifts (talents), but there is a time for everything. If you feel overwhelmed after asking God for grace, maybe you're just not giving yourself grace.

Psalms 46:5, "God is within her she will not fall."

Day 2

Beyond the Bubble

Romans 8:31b, "If God is for us, who can be against us?"

Have you ever been to a children's museum where there was a bubble you could stand in? You had to stand in this certain area and pull up strings soaked in the bubble liquid. I took my children to one of those places during my husband's deployments. They had so much fun getting inside and popping the bubble.

I'm sharing you this little story because sometimes, we military wives, when we get to a new location we just want to stay inside our comfort zone, our house or our bubble. If you've moved more than once you know it never gets easier to leave the friends you've made, and you don't want to set yourself up for that same hurt anymore. It's a natural response we have. You have an incredible life story though, you were meant to step out and be a light, not hide inside your bubble. You are meant to help those around you, to help them to know more about Jesus and maybe introduce them to Jesus for the first time. You have a ministry. We are all called to make disciples, to reach those hurting, to bring the comfort of Jesus. To minister and sharpen each other. Jesus loves you so much and he wants you to show others His love. I know it's easy to stay in your bubble, but let's try not to be selfish with what God has given us. It's not all about making friends but it is about helping others make eternal decisions. You are meant to do so much more than just sit in you. You have so much in you that others need to see. They need to see how you, a Godly woman of God handles a deployment or a crazy neighbor. Shine your light, girl! I know it can be a little nerve racking to try to make new friends every few years, but don't be fearful of the unknown, God has you.

When we moved to Marine Corps Air Station Kaneohe Bay, I was a little annoyed (to be honest) to meet new families. I loved my neighbors back in California and missed them as well as our wonderful church, but God quickly taught me that the only way I could share Christ love was to step outside of my front door and start meeting people again. It wasn't too long after moving that we had started to make forever friends again and even opening our home up for life group.

The new places we are placed in can be a little overwhelming, but take courage, God is with you. He will give you the right things to say. He will give you courage to poke your bubble and shine your light!

"The sooner you step away from your comfort zone; the sooner you'll realize that it really wasn't all that comfortable." –Eddie Harris Jr.

Day 3

You're Different… Right?

Galatians 5:15, "But God, who set me apart from my mother's womb and called me by His grace, was pleased."

I was standing in the check-out lane at the MCX when the little girl behind me said to her mom, "Mom I really want it! I want to be different! Everyone has it!" I thought to myself, "How can you want something in order to be different when everyone has it or is doing it?" Well...you can't (I hope you're rolling your eyes like I am). You have gifts, talents, and a personality that's completely yours. Own it and own it well! Be a trend setter—stop yourself from taking the easy route in going with the flow.

How do we choose to go with the flow as a military spouse? (Here's a few examples.)

- By choosing to talk the same way as those who do not have a personal relationship with Jesus.

- By choosing to act the same way as your non-married friends do while your husband is away training or deployed.
- By choosing to yell at your children like a short-tempered parent.

Do you see a trend here? <u>You Choose.</u> The choice is yours (Deut 30:14-20).

What makes you different from the world? What is it about the way you live that makes people think about how they are living? We are in this world, but we are not of it. In Romans 12:2 it says, "Do not conform to the pattern of this world, but be transformed by the renewing of your mind."

If you are doing the same thing as your unsaved neighbor who doesn't have a personal relationship with Jesus, are you different? Going to church doesn't make you a Christian any more than wearing a uniform makes you a member of the military. If you know something is wrong and you still do it with the knowledge that God will forgive you, it is sin plain and simple.

It's so easy to allow ourselves to get caught up in the gossip circle, but if we truly believe we have a personal relationship with Jesus we need to be different so that others will be drawn to God-- not away from Him. When you make the choice to be different, to lead rather than follow, God sees your commitment. He sees you making the choice to be different than the world around you and in doing so you are honoring Him.

"Being a Christian is more than just an instantaneous conversion- it is a daily process whereby you grow to be more and more like Christ."

-Billy Graham

Day 4

Passion

Deuteronomy 7:6b, "The Lord your God has chosen you out of all the peoples on the face of the earth to be his people, his treasured possession."

What is the one thing you wanted to do before someone told you it was impossible? You, my friend, have a special calling on your life. You may not remember what once made you excited to get up in the morning. The world has a way of diluting your enthusiasm, causing you to rethink the dream God gave you. I can confidently assure you the plan God had for you in the beginning is the same plan God still has for you now. God is not wishy washy and he has unlimited resources. Even though some obstacles have gotten in the way of the fulfillment, it doesn't mean God forgot what He created you to do. God's plan is not only for you, but also for your family! When you take the first step with passion, God says, "She is as ready as I have been. Let us continue this work." That step is putting action to your confession of faith. It opens the doors for God to pour out his goodness. It allows him to make great things happen that are not possible by our own planning or natural abilities. God gets so excited when He sees you doing exactly what He meant for you to be doing.

The negative voices will come from all over: strangers, the news, or even those who you are close to. Those voices are meant to bring you down, but I've learned I must quickly cast down the negative things I hear about me or my family. I do so by reminding myself that God is on my side and He is working all things out for my good because He loves me (Romans 8:28).

After being married and having children you may feel a little tired by all the things you are juggling. It's easy to forget about who we once were before our fun adventure as wife and mom started. For me, it takes a lot of internal arguments to convince myself that I need to do something that I am passionate about. Believe me, I have tons of passion for my husband and kiddos, however; I reached a point after our third baby was born that I realized I truly needed to also be doing something for me. Something that made me excited. God revealed to me that when you are happy and energized by doing things that you find thrilling, you have more to pour into your family. For me, it can be as simple as a fun workout or drinking a cup of coffee. Put your confidence in God and He will help you get your passion back to perform at your fullest potential in the areas he created just for you.

"When you attach passion to your dream, you get yourself closer to achieving it."

–Bob Kennedy

Day 5

Help Mate

Genesis 2:18, "The Lord God said, "It is not good for the man to be alone. I will make a helper suitable for him. "

You are your husband's helpmate. God gave you every tool you need to help your husband through every new adventure you go through as a military family. Remember the story from the Bible when Moses needed Aaron and Hur to hold his arms up (Exodus 17:12)? To make a long story short, Moses was tired and the Israelites would only win the battle while his arms were raised. Can you imagine holding your arms up for a whole entire deployment? Think of your husband after a long day. I know some wives say their husband doesn't work as hard as us because we're home with the kiddos and all that goes into building a healthy household. You need to put yourself in their boots for a second. He has challenges thrown at him non-stop. If it's not his higher ups looking for more out of him, it's the guys below him looking for guidance. I know at times it is hard to be a military wife. If you are like me, you've been doing countless and repetitive chores such as folding laundry, changing diapers, and/or cleaning up after fur-babies, but here's where we can kick it up a notch! Let's look at our husband as he comes through the door and say, "Dinner is ready, and we wanted to wait for you." I promise that your husband will be blown away by your effort and love for him. Being there for your husband is like lifting up his arms after a long day. While I know it is challenging, the effort you put into your marriage, the love you give to your husband, will only make your marriage stronger.

Let me pray with you:

Dear God, I pray that you will give my friend the strength she needs to advance her husband. I speak life into their marriage, and I thank you for everlasting love in their marriage that only comes from you. Please help my friend become the wife you've called her to be. Thank you for renewing her joy every day and for bringing even more passion into their marriage. I pray that when the world sees her marriage and asks how she's so close to her husband, she'll be able to testify and give thanks to you. We thank you for this and give you all the glory.

In Jesus' name, Amen.

Day 6

Intentional

Ephesians 5:10, "Carefully determine what pleases the Lord."

One day I asked my husband to give me one book to read that was military related. With a smirk he handed me, "A Message to Garcia" by Elbert Hubbard. One of the book's main points was for employees to take initiative at work. As I read the book, I couldn't help but think about our main mission on earth as Christians. In order for us to share the love of Jesus with others, we have to be intentional about why we believe what we believe.

When I think of the word intentional, I think about the choices I make and why I have made those choices. We have to be intentional about our daily actions. If we are intentional about our Christian walk, we will stand in the middle of craziness and not be moved by what we see (Colossians 1:23). We won't allow those doctor reports or rejection by others move us from sharing the love of Jesus. We will be intentional in every conversation, only judging ourselves by what we are talking about and if our thinking is right and pleasing to God. Relationships never just happen—we must be intentional! We have to be intentional about our relationship with God. Likewise, the same principles apply in marriage. You will not stay married for 25, 50, or 75 years if you never communicate with your spouse. Deployment is not an excuse to not communicate, after all, there is always snail mail. Living intentionally is not our natural reaction. Sometimes we have to change on purpose. A good relationship with God—and a good marriage—are two excellent reasons to change.

The opposite of being intentional in your decision making is to take a chance or risk. Sure, taking chances may sound like fun, especially the way Hollywood portrays them, but we are not to put any choice in the hands of chance (Matthew 6:33). Taking chances instead of seeking God first (His direction) in all our decisions is a sign of not fully surrendering to Him. Sometimes it's easier to sit back and let life happen around us. Today, let's remind ourselves we need to be intentional in our day to day lives. Let's allow our actions to point others to Him instead of away from Him.

"Change is inevitable. Growth is intentional."

–Glinda Cloud

Day 7

Stop the Drops!

Proverbs 27:15, "A quarrelsome wife is like the dripping of a leaky roof in a rainstorm;"

Drip

Drip

Drip

That's the sound our husband hears when we are constantly complaining or nagging. Annoying, isn't it? Believe me, I know. Being corrected by authority was okay to accept before I moved out of my parents' house, but it was a hard lesson to take when I found the Holy Spirit showing me that what I was really doing to my husband was nagging.

Did you know we as wives will either build up or break down our husband? It's true. As women of the home, we set the mood meter. We either make our home feel peaceful or stressful. When my husband, Samuel, and I were newly married, I didn't understand all the late nights and early mornings he would be at work. Growing up, I saw my dad go to work. He would leave early in the morning, but he was back by dinner time. To not see Samuel in the morning and then sometimes not until eight o'clock at night, I couldn't believe he was really working that long. I would ask him, "Why does it take you so long to get home?" Samuel would have the saddest look on his face when I would ask him that. I just couldn't understand until I had a moment with God during my devotion time. He showed me I was breaking down my husband's love for me when I questioned him as if he was doing something dishonest. The next day, I changed how I approached Samuel. I stopped questioning and showed him I was excited he was home. He looked so surprised the first time I did it and to this day my welcoming, along with our children's, puts a smile on his face.

Friend, we need to encourage our husband! When we become our husband's greatest cheerleaders, something will arise on the inside of him to help motivate him in the advancement of his own life. The advancing he does at work is your advancing. You encouraged him daily and now you both can enjoy the sweet rewards together. We can be our husband's biggest fans! Remember why you were so in love with him from the beginning and multiply that affection now since he is yours forever.

I've seen what a great wife can do to her husband when she helps him advance in all areas from work to family life. Sadly, I've also seen the evidence of a husband not getting that helpful support. When he gets torn down and disrespected at home, it frequently leads to losing jobs and a poor relationship with his family. This man has no major goals—only wishful dreams.

Let's choose today to advance our hubbies. Let's stop the drops by showing him more love and respect. The choice is yours to...

Encourage

Encourage

Encourage

"Of all the home remedies, a good wife is best."

-Kim Hubbard

Day 8

Field Day

Psalms 139:23, "Search me, God, and know my heart; test me and know my anxious thoughts."

There are going to be days when we just want to play, but then there is going to be those times when yes, we could play, but really we need to clean up. In all the military branches there are designated days where the military members have to perform janitorial work in areas around their barracks or work spaces. In the Marine Corps, they call it "field day".

When we were newly married, Samuel would let me know when he had to go help with field day. I remember on one such occasion I was excited for him and said, "Oh! That will be a fun day!" He gave me an awful look, "Really?" he said with such disgust. I asked him, "Isn't field day a fun activity day with games and food to celebrate your hard work? I had those at the end of every school year when I was young." That's when I learned field day in the military isn't the fun and games that

I remembered from my past. Look at how different those two things are. Cleaning verses playing games.

In the same way, if we never focus on looking inside us and seeing where there is need for a cleanup, sadly our lives may not be reflecting Christ. I realize cleaning may not be your favorite thing, but it's a necessity when it comes to keeping a healthy heart. If we keep on living our life the same way with the same routines; i.e. same words being used and same feelings, than we won't move any further in our faith. Where there is no change, there is no growth. Consequently, not performing a heart check will cause us to keep having the same results: feeling stuck.

If we are honest with ourselves, we each have things that we know we need to work on. Maybe it's our eating habits or holding on to past hurts. You can start performing a heart check by going to God and He will show us the necessary adjustments that need to be made in order to move forward into the plans He has for us. By asking God for help, we are doing our part and He will take care of the rest by helping you through the cleaning process. Sometimes this correction comes through channels we must be willing to hear from. Sometimes it is through our pastor, a friend, and sometimes it is even through our spouse. It can be through a show on television, or a life event. God is not limited in how He can choose to speak to you. We must be open to hear the need for change no matter the source.

When it is hard to accept, think of the greater purpose. When our hearts are cleaned, our actions will also become cleaner. Our main goal as a spouse and a mom is to become more and more like Christ and who He wants us to be. We can only become Christ-like if we turn our hearts to Him and ask that He show us those areas in which we need to improve. God will not throw this list at you and say you need to have all 71 things cleaned up in a month. No. He is a good father and He will walk you through each area of improvement only as you are capable of making the change and moving on to the next step in your journey.

Today, ask God to search your heart and listen closely to what He has to say.

Psalms 51:10, Create in me a clean heart, O God. Renew a loyal spirit within

me."

Day 9

It's Your Mountain

Habakkuk 3:19, "The Sovereign Lord is my strength; He makes my feet like the feet of a deer, He enables me to tread on the heights."

I was at a spin class at the base gym, pushing myself as hard as I could move those foot pedals when my instructor yelled out, "It's your mountain. It's your climb!" I immediately knew I needed to write that phrase down after class. What my sweet instructor wanted us to do was increase the resistance on our bikes so we would push harder with our legs to build strength. What she didn't know is she set something off in my spirit. The mountain that's in front of you is your mountain. The same mountain you have isn't the exact same as your best friend's, it's yours. The mountain is there for you to climb. When you climb that mountain, if it's a mountain of transitioning or a dream unfulfilled, whatever that mountain is to you, when you overcome it you will have strength you never thought possible. It is when you have climbed your mountain that you can press into a greater freedom. Don't misunderstand me, friend. God does not let mountains be in our way that he knows we cannot overcome. He is an all loving God. Everything he does or allows will be used for good. Sometimes we make those mountains more of a struggle then they need to be by the choices that we make. We are not robots. God gave us free will and sometimes we abuse that freedom and act in our own selfish ways, but God is always bigger than the mountain, even the mountains we make.

When our children were all school aged I decided I would jump back into the school world too. I decided to take some online classes towards an associate's degree in order to become a Teacher's Assistant. I was excited to start, but also very nervous. During the classes online, I did very well, but there was this test I was completely nervous about. So much so that I put it off for a whole year. After much procrastination I studied as best as I could and asked God to help bring those things to remembrance that I studied for. The test was definitely my mountain during that school period. By then I had learned I could only go over that mountain with God's help. When I completed and passed the test I had more confidence in myself then I did prior to taking the test, I knew God was my strength even for my education training.

Your faith is only as big as your last mountain. Do you have a mountain in front of you? Push up those sleeves and take it on. Will you sweat? Yes. Will you want to give up? Probably. But remember it's your mountain. Once you're over it, you're stronger, healthier, and more focused. You got this! Once you're over that mountain, you will see the promise fulfilled, the desire met. I'm excited for you! Remember…It's your mountain!

"Every mountain top is within reach if you just keep climbing."

—Barry Finlay

Day 10

Refresh

Proverbs 11:25, "A generous person will prosper; whoever refreshes others will be refreshed."

As a mom of three young children, it is rare that I have any quiet time or place. For me, not even our bathroom is a quiet place.

When our husband leaves for work, whether he has a 30 minute drive or just a 10 minute drive because you live close, he can use that time to refresh and shake off whatever the day threw at him. As wives, some of us are home with the kiddos all day. Some of us have jobs and some of us even take our kiddos with us to our jobs. Whatever your situation, it can be harder for moms to have that kind of moment to get refreshed.

When we lived in Hawaii, my fitness coach would say, "There is no such thing as a bad workout". I'm saying to you today, there is no such thing as a bad devotion time with God. You have made time for Him today---that's huge!

God sees you have your hands full with your family. If you're standing in the kitchen reading this as you are also making lunches for your family or if you are reading this on your lunch break. I want you to take a deep breath and breathe out. Say to God "I need your grace today because it's not about me. It's about the lives I can impact for you today." You are at this duty station and in this community for more than yourself.

Friend, believe me, my three children were once little ones. I know days can be a challenge, but in the Bible Jesus talks about refreshing. Even Jesus went away to pray, to get away from the distractions of his life. Don't feel guilty for needing some "me time." You can be the mommy and the wife you are called to be better, but only when you take time to be with Jesus.

When you become refreshed, you can better pour into your husband and children. Take a moment to quiet your mind and heart. Even if it's just three minutes to pray. Ask God to give you grace for today and thank him for what He's both doing and going to do through you. It's in these quiet times with God that He will often give us the strength we need for this calling He has placed inside of us... inside of you.

"When we draw near to God, our minds are refreshed and our strength is renewed."

–Our Daily Bread

Day 11

Good to Go

Hebrews 13:21, "May he equip you with all you need for doing his will. May he produce in you, through the power of Jesus Christ, every good thing that is pleasing to Him. All glory to him forever and ever! Amen."

I never knew "good to go" was a military phrase until one of Samuel's friends pointed it out after I said it to my husband. He looked at my husband and said (laughingly), "Wow! Your wife is brainwashed."

As Christians we need to constantly be good to go. Good to go meaning: prepared for use. When things are thrown at us and the world around us is shaking their heads, your confession should be "I am good to go." You will be good to go because you are equipped for anything. You've got this because God has you.

When we moved from Hawaii to North Carolina, we experienced a bit of culture shock. I had to keep reminding myself that God has my family. Even though adjusting is typically a challenge, I knew God already put the tools within me to help us adjust quickly. When you first move to any new location, I can't promise you that you'll love it right away. The local community usually looks at you with interest (sometimes not in the best way). They don't understand why you don't dress like or sound like them. One day after the beginning of a new school year our oldest son's teacher called me into the class to talk about how Elijah was talking. I was a little worried before the meeting, but then when she told me that she was worried he kept saying "Ya" instead of "Yes" the pressure was immediately released. I proceeded to calmly let her know we had just moved here from Hawaii, and in Hawaii they commonly use the term "Ya" instead of "Yes" as a term locally acceptable. I explained to her that he had picked that word up (we all really did) and we were trying to not use it as frequently in the new community we had relocated to. She thought that was interesting information and better understood his habit. Consequently, after living in North Carolina for only 3 years, my children and I caught ourselves frequently saying, "y'all", commonly used there. Trust me, if you haven't experienced it already, you too will find it interesting the sayings and actions you can pick up from different places you have lived due to military moves.

God is with you wherever the military sends you. God is always with you wherever He sends you while with the military. As a child of God, we truly have to believe that even though your husband's monitor says you need to move to a certain location, God is the one who needs you there. If God needs you there, believe me,

He will supply you with all the wisdom you need to live there. When you move you may be tempted to think "Seriously God. How could you send us here?!" Friend, you just have to trust (fully trust) that He has you. He won't leave you just because there isn't a *Wi-Fi* connection. You will always be good to go because you know He has you.

Looking back, I truly know it was God who sustained me over the years by His grace. Whatever is going on in your world, big or small, don't forget that God is with you. He will give you the grace you need in each situation. God will enable you with the right dose of grace for that trial. He is with you and His grace is yours.

Let me pray with you:

Dear Lord, I pray for my friend today that you will give her a good to go mentality so she will be ready to go when she needs to go. I thank you Lord for giving her favor in every area of this military life. Give her wisdom for the upcoming move or deployment. No matter what may g her way. Thank you Jesus that she is good to go in you.

In Jesus' name, Amen.

Day 12

Focus!

James 1:8, "Such a person is double-minded and unstable in all they do."

If you're focused, you are not double minded. When I was six years old, my dream was to become a wife and a mommy. I knew exactly what I wanted for my life for when I grew up. My first dream came true when I became a wife in 2004, then my dream to become a mommy started coming true in 2006. By 2015, all three of our children were of school age. I was beyond crushed when our last child entered kindergarten. Jill, one of my military sisters came over to our house to chat. I was so sad when I told her, "My dream was to become a wife and a mommy. Now they're all in school and don't need me! Now what?" Jill looked at me, smiled and said (in her very bubbly tone), "Katherine, it's time to dream a new dream." When she said that to me it was like a light went off on the inside of me. I took what she said to God asking "Now what...what do I do with my time?" He gently said, "Finish the devotional." It had been such a long time since I thought about this devotional. He had put it on my heart to write it years earlier, but life had slowed the process. Now that I had more time, I began to focus more on my prayer time. Recognizing both my time in prayer and the experiences I had gained as contributing to my knowledge and ability to best be used by Him. Apparently, it hadn't been God's plan for me to write it quickly. I learned so much over those years since He originally gave me the dream.

When a dream you have becomes a reality such as in my case where it didn't happened until after my children didn't require my full attention anymore, God can renew the dreams He gave you from the past. He can remind you of what you need to do to fulfill your destiny in Him.

Your dream is for you! You may not have cheerleaders walking behind you every day cheering you on, but you still need to encourage yourself. Take ownership of your dream and stay focused. Listen for God's voice in everything you do and everywhere you go. He is the one who will keep you on track. Let me tell you a little recognized fact, when your dream seems unreachable, you're probably on the right track. If you could reach the dream in your own strength, it can't be a God given dream. Why? Because in a God given dream you will need God's help to get you to the dream fulfilled. That's the only way He gets the glory. He wants a relationship with us. How can we be pressed for a relationship if we are doing it all on our own? (Turn to the back of this book and find the "Vision" Page." There you can write exactly what God is speaking to you about your dreams and you can refer to it whenever you need a reminder.)

Proverbs 3:5-12, "Trust God from the bottom of your heart; don't try to figure out everything on your own. Listen for God's voice in everything you do, everywhere you go; he's the one who will keep you on track. Don't assume that you know it all. Run to God! Run from evil! Your body will GLOW with health, your very bones will VIBRATE with life!" The Message Bible

Day 13

Old Ways

Isaiah 34:16, "... Forget about what's happened; don't keep going over old history. Be alert, be present. I'm about to do something brand-new. It's bursting out! Don't you see it? There it is!" The Message Bible

Feeling stuck today? Not liking the results of your choices from yesterday (I know I've felt like that)?

When my husband and I were newly married, I worked as a receptionist. There was one occasion I remember quite well. I made an awful mistake by over committing myself. Consequently, I wasn't able to show up for a women's tea function that would be held over the weekend. When Monday came around, and I had to return to work my boss brought me in his office and told me I was a "flake". I started crying and apologized for not attending. I had made a mistake, but I didn't let that one mistake allow me from never signing up for events. I learned from that moment to not over commit my time and to commit myself only to things I knew I could do. You know that old saying, "Don't make a promise you can't keep."

If you have a hard time letting go of wrong choices you've made in life, this is meant for you...

Forgive yourself. It's time to move on!

We all make bad choices in life, even if it's just over indulging at Thanksgiving dinner (or Thanksgiving dessert…yum). Even though I have over indulged myself during dinner and felt completely awful the next day that does not give me the right to keep reminding myself how awful of a person I am. Reminding myself of my mistake will not cause me to change my eating habits. Notice I chose to say "...make bad choices..." as in: you will continue to make bad decisions throughout your life. God knows. He doesn't want you to remain stuck in disappointment and depression because of it. He forgives and forgets if you seek Him and give it to Him through repentance.

The times I've completely messed up have helped me avoid situations later that would have caused me the same grief.

If you've asked God to forgive you for a past mess up, He has forgiven you. Did you hear me? He has forgiven you already, so forgive yourself. Yes, you had a mess up, but now you can take the results of the mess up and prevent it from happening again. Let yourself off the hook.

Regret from your old ways will keep you from walking through the new doors God has opened for you. If you keep replaying the bad; the hurts; the disobedience, sadly you will never move past your past. So let's agree together we will move past our past starting today!

"Old ways won't open new doors."

-*Mark Strand*

Day 14

Hurry!

Psalms 27:14, "Wait for the Lord; be strong and take heart and wait for the Lord..."

Have you heard the expression "hurry up and wait"? (I'm sure you're laughing because you've heard too much of that saying.)

Waiting can be overwhelming, but take rest in your Heavenly Father. He will give you the strength while you're waiting. Waiting for what? You know how it goes: waiting for orders to see where you're going to move next; waiting to see if your husband is selected for promotion; or waiting to see if you got the house on base (in the neighborhood you wanted). The list goes on and on when you're in the military.

No matter how hard or challenging waiting seems, you've waited for the answers to come before and you can do it again. Unpleasant? Yes, but you got this. While I know it's unpleasant to wait, don't give up!

When we were waiting on our next orders while we were stationed on Camp Pendleton, we honestly thought we would get orders to move to North Carolina (North Carolina would put us closer to our families in Michigan). When we finally received our orders, we were a little disappointed at first. As you can imagine, we were also completely shocked when they were instead for Kaneohe Bay, Hawaii. We were even more shocked to find out we had less than a month to do this very big move. The stress level shot through the roof. It took us a while to accept it, but we knew God was over this move just as He had been over us through every little and major adventure.

Waiting for the orders made us realize how much we needed God to direct us, to prepare us for what was unknown to us.

If you are waiting for a doctor's report to come in, waiting for your husband to return, or waiting to "have this baby already!" Cling to God. He knows and sees your heart. He sees you having that restless sleep. Ask God to help you get peaceful sleep tonight. Take your anxious heart and surrender it to God. He wants you to rest in Him while you wait.

Let me pray with you:

Dear Lord, I know you see my friend's anxious heart as she waits. I pray you would give her peace like no other. Thank you for the grace you're pouring into her even now. Thank you, Jesus, for her and for all she does for her family. We love you Lord, and thank you for loving us first.

In Jesus' name, Amen.

John 14:27, "Peace I leave with you; my peace I give you. I do not give to you as the world gives. Do not let your hearts be troubled and do not be afraid."

Day 15

Don't Blink

Isaiah 66:3a, "As a mother comforts her child, so will I comfort you;"

This is for all the mamas out there. Days may seem long when you are cleaning up throw up; wiping faces; potty training your toddler while holding your other infant; carpooling; cleaning up dog messes; taking kiddos to doctors and making meals for everybody. However, when the children are grown and on their own, you will laugh and cherish those crazy, lack of sleep (lack of shower) days. I promise you.

In 2015, the last of our three children became school-aged. I packed the summer before they started school full of fun activities, but honestly I had a very hard time emotionally that summer. Our youngest would enter kindergarten, and she had always been home with me. In fact, I hadn't been in a position to be home by myself for over nine years. For a time I had cleaned homes professionally and she would come with me. When I had also worked as a nanny prior to having children until well after, my kiddos went to work right along with me. We had so much fun together, and I was so sad that time was ending. Looking back, I still get choked up about it. Now our youngest has completed kindergarten and I see how much she enjoys learning at school.

Mamas, when I came home from the hospital with our first child, I knew that despite the sleepless nights, it would all pass by too quickly. Now with all three in school, I'm so glad I didn't get upset about the little things like laundry, dishes, late night feedings and paying bills (This list could go on and on). Cherish all of it! All you have and are doing now will soon be a distant memory (and hopefully one with lots of photos).

I wish I could hug you right now because I know some days are harder than you think you can manage. I know you have the strength and grace in you, though! Please know, you are the best mommy for your child(ren) and you are beyond qualified to be a wife and mother. You were born to be a mom and a wife, so please don't doubt yourself. Keep on loving your husband and your babies. As you comfort and nurture your children, Jesus will comfort you. When you're tired, Jesus will pour his strength into you. You got this! Take a deep breath and know that you're right where you should be and only you can love your family the way they need to be loved.

"The days are long but the years are short."

–Gretchen Rubin

Day 16

Pretty You, Ugly Heart

1 Samuel 16: 7, "But the Lord said to Samuel, 'Do not consider his appearance or his height, for I have rejected him. The Lord does not look at the things people look at. People look at the outward appearance, but the Lord looks at the heart.'"

How many times have you heard someone say, "I had a great workout!"? Now, how many times have you heard someone say, "I had such a great devotion time with God this morning!"? You've probably heard the fitness example more than the "churchy" answer. My incredible parents and my awesome in-laws are fortunate to be surrounded by people of the same faith. My parents have had some of their closest, Godly friends for over 30 years. My in-laws have always worked and contributed personal time to their church for about the same amount of time. Relating this back to our military life, let's be real, many of our friends move before even the third year of us really getting to know them. As we walk through this military life, it is common for us to talk with each other about our fitness (or failed attempts at fitness). Our conversations typically revolve around injuries, someone's spouse getting "taped in" (for body fat standards) or what work-out plan we are trying out.

Others may see our lack of education, our weight; or who has the most popular haircut. God sees our hearts. I know your life is busy but you still have to ask yourself, "Am I spending as much time in God's presence as I do on my own image?" I know that is a hard question to ask. Let's take a moment to think about that.

If we are not spending time in God's Word our insides will more than likely become dry.

Believe me, I enjoy a good workout, but I'm hopelessly lost without my devotion time with God. Remember: we can look so awesomely fit, but our insides can be screaming out for God. His presence allows you to be renewed by Him. It's one thing to have clarity during a yoga class, but my fit friend, it's a whole other thing to have God's power cleanse you. You will find out that same urge you feel to go on a good run you will also feel when you have a routine of an alone time with God. It's amazing to see Him change us from the inside out. Let's get fit in Him.

"Focus on what you want your life to look like. Not just your body."

-Sarah Faille

Day 17

Strong Faith

Proverbs 16:3, "Commit to the Lord whatever you do, and he will establish your plans."

When God gives you a dream in your heart to do something big whether it involves opening a coffee shop, becoming a teacher, designing a new product, or even finishing high school to receive your GED. God will never have a Plan B for your life. Sometimes we settle too soon or refuse to step into His plan. I promise that our way is never as good as His way. Stick with the first plan God has for you! It may look scary, seem challenging, look ugly in the first stages, and make you want to scream; however, it's the best plan for you.

A good example of committing to a plan is what history records say about Hernan Cortes in 1519. As a Spanish conquistador, Hernan and his fleet of ships arrived in the Americas to conquer the native people and obtain land. He knew his crew was few in numbers and chance of success was small, so he ordered his men to "burn the boats." The idea was that the boats represented their escape from whatever trouble was ahead. Essentially, Cortes burned Plan B, forcing the crew to commit 100 percent of their focus to their conquest, as their lives now fully depended on that success. It's time to burn the boats in your life.

Do you have a backup plan for everything? Stop! When God gives you a plan, even if it's a small plan, run with it! Allow yourself to give it all you got, and then God can do His part. For example, if you know God is telling you to get up a few minutes earlier to pray and do some Bible reading every day you could make endless excuses and brush it off. Don't! Think about the possibilities of what your obedience can effect: your children to succeed at school, receiving that job you wanted, your husband advancing in his career, your health to improve, or even a family relationship to have reconciliation.

By saying "nah" to the small plan, you are also saying "nah" to the fantastic plan God has designed for you. I promise you, when you commit to take that first step with 100% faith, doors will open. The things you see as setbacks are really things that push you forward. When you say yes to God, He says, "She is ready for the next step." It is in our obedience that our potential becomes reality. Our dreams can only become reality after we take the first step! When God puts something in your heart, He will walk with you each step of the way.

"Spirit, lead me where my trust is without borders and my faith will be made stronger in the presence of my savior."

—Hillsong, Young & Free

Day 18

Pressure

Isaiah 40: 31, "But those who hope in the Lord will renew their strength."

The pressure in our household can hit a high note as those deployment deadlines approach. When we feel this pressure we must first ask God for the strength to handle it, then the grace and wisdom to handle it in love.

When my family moved from base housing to a home off base in southern California, there was so much that needed to be done to that house. From installing new flooring to remodeling the kitchen, the major projects were piled up and my two little boys didn't understand why they couldn't run free around the house. About a month into the move we had family planning to visit and I also found out I was pregnant. As excited as I was about being pregnant, I was overwhelmed with our living conditions. The pressure to get things in order, livable and prepared for guests made me extremely frustrated. Looking back, I still shake my head and know the only way I got through that stage was Jesus. Even though the surrounding things were insane, I knew God could bring the peace I needed. Each morning I asked Him, "God, please give me the grace I need for today." He truly did answer my prayer. When the pressures is on, go to Him and ask Him to give you the grace to get through your crazy situation.

I know deadlines need to be met, children need to be fed, dogs need to be walked, deployments have to happen, and litter boxes need to be cleaned. In all the busyness we can choose to take it to God. Let's allow ourselves to get so caught up in the things of God by listening to worship, watching sermons online, and reading the Bible that when life's pressures get so high, our faith will be even higher. As hard as it is to share this with you, sometimes the pressures are meant to sharpen us and equip us with experiences to share with someone else later in life, to encourage each other that God will always be with us. When pressures rise, go to God for strength.

"A diamond is a piece of coal under pressure. If you are feeling pressure you are about to shine."

-Victoria Osteen

Day 19

Deployed but Not Alone

Isaiah 41:10, "Do not fear, for I am with you; do not anxiously look about you, for I am your God. I will strengthen you, surely I will help you, and surely I will uphold you with my righteous right hand."

When my husband's deployment approaches, I hold close to this verse.

Don't worry sweet friend, as the deployment approaches, God has some awesome things lined up for both of you during this time. When my husband deploys, my prayer is always, "God, thank you that there is no time or distance in the spirit. Thank you, that even though we are far apart, we will become closer to you and to each other." You may be saying, "How can we become closer to each other when we are away from each other?" My husband and I learn a lot about each other during each deployment. We see the areas we both need to work on individually and take the time to work on ourselves. We make the changes and God speaks to us on how we can be a better husband and wife and we share with each other what those things are.

It's truly amazing what God can do when you invite Him to be the center of your marriage, especially during a deployment. When you invite God into all the loneliness a deployment can bring into your home, God shows up and shows off. In 2014, we were approaching our fourth deployment, and I prayed the prayer mentioned above. I knew God would direct both our steps even when physically separate from each other. Sure enough, when he returned home we both felt closer to each other and to the plan God had for our family. When you can honestly say, "God, you see this deployment and all the separation that comes with it, but you're a good father. I know you will turn this around for good." God says, "That's my girl! She knows I will never leave her and I will continue to strengthen her and her marriage."

During the 2014 deployment with a MEU, my husband was part of a men's Bible study group. When he returned home, the same guys from the MEU Bible study came to our home for more study time. It was beyond anything I could have ever thought to see our home filled with young Marines and their wives digging deeper in their faith. As your next deployment or workup approaches, remember God has you both and no matter what you're facing, you are not alone.

"Let your faith be bigger than your fear."

–Unknown Author

Day 20

Muddy

Hebrews 10:35, "So do not throw away this confident trust in the Lord. Remember the great reward it brings you!"

Progress isn't always obvious. Do you feel like you're in a constant run through mud where you feel like you keep pushing harder than it should be? On the other side of that mud pond is your dream. If that's you today don't quit.

I've had this struggle before. I felt I was constantly being pulled one way or another. When we moved to North Carolina, I was entering the biggest transition of my life. All my children would be full time students, my husband's new squadron and would be in and out for a year and a half. I started experiencing weird health problems. All my symptoms pointed to Lyme disease. I pushed that aside and knew I had to stand on God's word to get through the doctor's report. Needless to say, within 6 months all the symptoms went away. Praise God! At that time in my life, I felt like the pressure was on and I was constantly pushing through that difficult mud bog of my own life. It honestly felt like nothing good was going on in my life. I couldn't figure it out and I finally took it to God. I asked Him to do a work in me that only He could do. I asked Him to give me peace during this major transition. I felt better after going to God. Did everything turn around the next day? No it didn't, but I can clearly see I am now stronger than I was before.

We all sometimes walk through a muddy time in our lives, but we just have to keep pushing. We must keep the faith and know that at the end of that struggle, our arms will be stronger and so will our faith. The end result will be our dream fulfilled.

Make your mind up now that you won't quit! You have fought too hard for too long to give up now. What if tomorrow is your breakthrough? Don't allow the enemy to talk you out of what you know your assignment is.

What do we do when we're peaceful and we know we are in good hands? We fall asleep soundly. Don't let the problems going on around you steal your sleep and your peace. Don't forget, when you have had enough and you feel like you can't do it anymore, that's the perfect place to be. You are totally reliant on God and He will take over from there.

Take a deep breath. Have childlike faith and know that the end result is going to work out in your favor.

"Small progress is still progress."

–Unknown Author

Day 21

Praise On

Psalms 34:1, "I will honor the Lord at all times. His praise will always be in my mouth."

You know when you make coffee and the smell fills up the room? You know that coffee will be delicious and the thought makes your toes curl (and if you're a non-coffee drinker, the smell of coffee probably makes your toes curl for a different reason). Now think of that thought but replace it with Jesus. Do you know what brings the presence of God? Our praise! When you make praise part of your everyday life, and not just something you do at church, you are welcoming Jesus to be with you. Unlike the temporary enjoyment of a good cup of coffee, there's never ending joy in Jesus' presence.

There was a mighty battle so epic the Bible called it Perez Uzza or "God burst upon Uzza" (1Chronicles 13:1-14). When we allow God to be present in our lives, there is a BURST that takes place in the spiritual. Things that once pulled you back will not be allowed to touch you because God's presence brings a burst into that situation!

When we were stationed in Hawaii, Samuel and I were in need of that burst of God's presence in our lives. We just wanted to see more of God at work in us and through us. As you know, when your husband is in the military there are many challenges that seem so overwhelming many resort to drinking and other things that are self-destructive in nature. We knew we needed more than our everyday devotions. We enjoyed serving and going to church, but we wanted more of God. Our church was amazing, and they offered discipleship classes. One class was about praise and how it brings His presence. When we began to praise and worship God with singing as part of our daily lives, we could feel a freshness come into our home by making such a simple choice. When you choose to praise God no matter what is going on in your world (i.e. PCS to a place you didn't want, or something as frustrating as fraudulent bank account charges), you are bringing Him into the crazy mix of whatever is happening. He will bring His presence, the very peace of God, into your situation. God will see your heart not moved by what is going on and how you still praise Him no matter the craziness. Take a deep breath and don't forget to keep your praise on.

Psalms 59:17, "O my Strength, to you I sing praises, for you, O God, are my refuge, the God who shows me unfailing love."

Day 22

Guide

2 Chronicles 16:8b, "Yet when you relied on the Lord, he delivered them into your hand."

Being part of the military, it's probable your husband has been required to perform some form of drill ceremony. Every drill team has a leader, a person responsible for giving direction as well as the pace of the march. Just like the men on the drill team rely on the leader for the next step, we can look to God for the next steps in our life. I know it's challenging sometimes, and we find ourselves wondering about our next steps. God is our source in all things, so He will lead us into the exact plan He has for us, if we will allow Him.

When we were stationed in California and before we had children, I was a nanny for a family of two little girls. The family decided they were going to be moving away so I needed to find a new nanny job. I asked God to help me find the right job that fit our family. Shortly after my husband left on deployment, I found out we were expecting a baby. When I went to my first checkup, the midwife Sarah, was so sweet and friendly. We talked a lot about children, and it even was brought up I was looking for a nanny job. To my surprise, Sarah was looking for a nanny for her girls because their daycare was closing. Sarah immediately asked me to interview at her home and meet her family. Shortly after that, I was hired on to be their nanny. The whole time I was with that family I couldn't have felt more loved at a work place than I did with them. To this day, we are still great friends. God will guide you in situations you can't even begin to imagine. He wants the best for you. When you ask Him for clear direction, He will lead you through each step of the process.

When you rely on Jesus, He will put the right people, right job, and even the right doctors into your life. If you're continually trusting in yourself or Google, you're trusting in your own strength, but when God directs you, watch out! So many opportunities will come your way.

Let me pray with you:

Dear Lord, I pray you will guide my friend. Thank you for all that you have planned for her life and her family's life. We thank you for favor after favor, blessing after blessing, to be established in her life today and throughout this year.

In Jesus' name, Amen

Day 23

Closer to Him

2 Chronicles 15:1a-2, "Then the Spirit of God came upon Azariah... The Lord will stay with you as long as you stay with him! Whenever you seek him, you will find him. But if you abandon him, he will abandon you."

When you get alone, or even when you're driving your crazy kiddos around, you can have a talk with God. Thanking Him, praising Him, asking Him for direction and seeing the results is how you build trust in God. When you pray, read the Word of God, and sing praises, it builds a stronger bond with Jesus. If you seek him, you will find him.

When we were stationed in California, there was a horrible helicopter crash on our base involving Marines my husband worked with. My husband was part of the crew to go observe the cleanup at the site and provide oversight. Can you imagine how hard it would be to observe the cleanup of a fatal crash? Our family grieved so much for the families that were involved, and I know my husband took it very hard. There was a moment when I was driving the kiddo's home from a fun mommy and me class. When I looked in the backseat and all three of them were asleep. I started to cry because I thought about the families who had lost loved ones. Their children wouldn't have moments like mine anymore because their mommy or daddy was gone. I asked God to show up and give me guidance what I could do to help my husband feel more loved and supported during times like this. As soon as I called out to God for help, I felt His peace, and I also felt that my husband simply needed an ear to listen and not to speak. I even felt I needed to make comfort foods for dinner that night. The same evening my husband opened up about his feelings about the accident and he told me my dinner made his day. Whenever I cry out to God during the tough times, I know He hears my voice and I can hear His too.

When you go after God and all that He has for you, He will reward you with His closeness. When He is close to you, the troubles that come will not frighten you because the knowledge God provides will come through for you once again.

"The closer we walk with God, the clearer we see His guidance."

- Unknown Author

Day 24

The Struggle is Real

1 John 4:4, "You, dear children, are from God and have overcome them, because the one who is in you is greater than the one who is in the world."

With every problem, I'm tempted to amplify my problem to my closet friend or my mom. It's just easier to talk to someone who can look at me and either help me solve the problem or say they are sorry for me. Friend, at what point do we surrender all to Jesus? At what point do we say to God "I just don't understand"? Sure, He doesn't always directly answering us back right away, but going to God FIRST will give you peace like no other. You'll either walk away from prayer time knowing what you need to do or you will have peace that the answer is soon to follow. As military wives, we walk through many tough times, but the military community is awesome at offering help. It's okay to take advantage of the many services the military offers as long as you recognize Jesus is the only one who brings true peace. He will provide the resource you need to press on. Just depend on Him and not the resource.

Do you remember the story in the eighth chapter of Matthew where Jesus falls asleep during the storm? Can you picture his frantic disciples living in today's world? They would be taking selfies with big waves behind them, hash-tagging "#thestruggleisreal". The disciples were scared enough to go wake Jesus up so there had to be some kind of talk amongst themselves before waking him up! I imagine Peter saying to John, "You go ask Him. I asked Him last time!" I wonder if the disciples, before waking Jesus, went over all of their missed opportunities in life, thinking this would be the end (Matt 8:23-27).

In the middle of a problem, do you amplify your problem or amplify God? When you make your problem bigger it means you can't stop thinking or talking about it. Instead of amplifying your problem, amplify God! Believe me, I may not have been through the same problem as you, but I have had my share of problems. Focusing too much on your problem is showing lack of trust in God.

God is with you, friend, in the middle of your storm. Remember to amplify Him instead of the problem, and God will show up and show off!

"Don't magnify your problem, magnify your God."

–Tony Evans

Day 25

Cry Out

Psalms 30:5, "...weeping may last through the night, BUT joy comes with the

morning."

Have you ever had an all-out cry? When the cry is so deep it doesn't just make your mascara run, it literally takes it away. In that moment, I'm a mess, but afterwards I am so thankful I lost it before my Heavenly Father. Sometimes, ladies, we just need an all-out cry. Remember when you were little and you would go crying to your mom or daddy? Well, that's how God wants us to come before Him, to depend on Him. He wants to make you feel better. When my husband leaves for deployments, I have about a week of random tears. The first and second day are the most hard on me and the children.

Friend, there are days when you will feel like you don't know how you are going to carry on, if it's not because of a deployment, it will be something else. Whatever is bringing on the storm, know its ok to cry. God has promised us He would work everything out for our good. Why? It's simple: He loves us. There will always be things that try bringing us down (maybe you're not understanding how you could be moving overseas when you finally made some friends on base), but we have to choose to trust God will work it out.

When we received our orders to PCS to Hawaii, I stayed positive, but I knew I was going to miss so much in California. We had a wonderful church, friends, and I absolutely enjoyed the neighbors we were blessed with. I didn't think I would ever adapt in Hawaii, but God had a plan and it was a great plan for us.

You may not understand why God is doing what He is doing, but trust in His plans just as you trust Him for everything else. God has you, friend, and His plans for you are beyond amazing. Take a moment, cry your eyes out, but remember that joy comes in the morning. God's "got" you.

"The strongest people in the morning are the people who cried all night."

– Unknown Author

Day 26

Physical Fitness Test

Ruth 1:16, "Where you go I'll go, where you stay I'll stay."

We all hear our hubbies talk about the next PFT being inconvenient, exhausting, or not the best of times. Did you know we as military wives go through this, too? Sure, we're not out there ripping out the pull ups (if you are, that's so awesome! You go girl!), but every new PCS move or career change is a new physical and emotional test. I'm not a fan of tests, though I love learning. When we move, we can choose to get bitter with our husband, the command, and even the President. In the opposite approach (and much more positive way), we can say "Let's do it!" My husband came home from work one day, and he looked completely wiped out. He said we needed to talk upstairs. By the way he looked I honestly thought someone passed away. He started by saying, "We are moving". I said, "Okay. Do you know where and when?" He took a deep breath, "We need to be in Hawaii in 25 days." It was my turn to take a deep breath. "Okay. We can do it." He looked completely shocked. "Really? I saw you taking this a lot worse." I told him, "It will all work out. There's no use in complaining because there's nothing we can do about it. Besides, we have a lot to do to get ready!"

I had trouble seeing how everything would come together, but we moved in 25 days! All military wives have a choice: Become crazy upset about every change or we can help our husband through the change.

Did you know when the Israelites crossed over the Red Sea it was the women who led the procession of praise and singing to the Lord? Ladies, during these physical and emotional tests we have to choose to be the cheerleaders in our homes. Military lives are crazy, but praising God will change the atmosphere in any situation. Let praise and a calm spirit guide you through the test. You, my friend, can set the tone for every new adventure. Feeling the pressure? Calm down! God is in you, so cling to the Word whenever you're confronted with your own PFT.

Psalms 121:2, "My help comes from the LORD, the Maker of heaven and earth."

Day 27

Stand Down

Matthew 23:11-12, "Do you want to stand out? Then step down. Be a servant. If you puff yourself up, you'll get the wind knocked out of you. But if you're content to simply be yourself, your life will count for plenty." The Message Bible

Stand down is a phrase in the military that means to take a relaxed posture from a former alert posture. When a military member assumes the stand down posture, it means everything is calm and okay.

We may allow ourselves to think grand thoughts whenever we take dinner to the guys in the barracks or a family with a new baby, however; if we do those sweet actions for our own recognition, God doesn't get the glory—you and I do. Sure, we did all the cooking and cleaning as well as put your kiddos in the cutest clothes, but what was your point? If you're not building someone else up while giving, God doesn't get the glory. God has placed creativity inside of you. Allow God to completely shine through all the parties you throw, and gifts given. Remember: God has graced you to encourage others and give other people ideas on how to stay fit at fifty or give generous gifts. Do you know God gets so much pleasure when He sees His children use the gifting He has put inside of us? He also loves it when His children say, "God is my source of creativity." You can do the things you can do because God placed those attributes inside of you.

Allow your amazing gifts to show people Jesus. You may be the only one showing Jesus to the people in your community! Even if you can throw it down at the gym or you quit that smoking habit, shine your light so others can see you didn't achieve it with your own strength, but the God who is in you did it! When God gets the glory, we can know that every seed of love we sow will grow into something beautiful. Know God will always bless you for giving Him the glory. All of our achievements on this earth will only be successful if they bring others with us to eternity. You can do what you do because God put that gifting into you. Work it girl and shine that light!

Acts 17:28a, "For in him we live and move and have our being."

Day 28

Meek Me

Matt 5:5, "...for the meek will inherit the earth."

I once had a dream that I was at a store and waiting in line for a return when the lady at the counter kept calling everyone behind me and skipping me! I was so furious in my dream, hands on the hip, attitude and the whole thing. When I approached the counter to "bring it", I was woken up! I was still so upset laying there in my bed thinking of what I would do and say if it had happened for real. I even said in my head, "If that really happened, I'd be like…" when I was interrupted by the very real voice of my Heavenly Father, "Would you really say that?" I tried to reason, "She was so wrong to do that to me." His voice said again, "So you would get upset with her?" "Well…" I tried. Then He said, "Katherine, you need to become meeker. You cannot move forward in your walk with me if you choose to react in your own way. No matter what someone does to you, and how mean they can be, choose to react in love." When I knew He had finished speaking, I quickly wrote the dream down. When I got up the next morning my husband said, "So God spoke to you last night, huh?" I said, "What? You heard his voice too?" He laughed, "No, I read your note."

Behind the scenes, my husband had been praying I would be calmer when it came to confrontation. While I never freaked out on him, I did with others. He saw that and had been praying for God to reveal it to me. I have never been one for confrontation, but I would always get worked up when someone wasn't being fair or truthful. When that dream was given to me, I took it as a helpful tip from God to work on my meekness level.

What are your reactions to unfair situations? Do you still remain calm and work through it in a Christ- like manner? I am not saying every day will be a joy and you'll never lose your cool. Becoming meeker is a process, but it will get easier as you allow the Holy Spirit to correct you. God's correction always changes you to look more like Him.

Let me pray with you:

Dear Jesus, please help us, as military wives, to stay calm under fire and in the midst of unfair situations. Help us shine the light no matter what our mind wants to do or say.

Thank you, Jesus. Amen.

Day 29

Christ Like

Philippians 3:12, "Not that I have already obtained this or am already perfect...,

because Christ Jesus has made me his own." English Standard Version

Jesus wants to use us in everyday situations. Not so you receive high fives, but so

others around you can know and see Jesus. It's not about being perfect, it's about

being more Christ like. By going out of your way to shine the light of Christ,

you're being a missionary wherever you are. Remember: God knew ahead of time

every place you would live.

I have a friend named Kelly, we were not always friends. In the beginning, I was

so sure Kelly didn't like me by her offhanded comments and eye rolls, even though

she and I had never spoken before. Our husbands worked together, we had another

mutual acquaintance and I sometimes saw her around the base shopping. I would

be friendly and greet her with a standard "Good morning" or "I like your outfit."

No matter how indifferently Kelly responded, I didn't say anything confrontational

back to her. It's a funny experience when God needs you to reach someone for

Him even when that individual isn't too thrilled about you. One season, Kelly's son ended up being on Elijah's soccer team. We ended up talking more and making an eventual connection, we even exchanged phone numbers. After soccer was over, both of our husbands were sent to a training school together. The school was very challenging on us as wives and for our husbands. I texted Kelly and encouraged her that she could get through this tough time away from her husband and that I was praying for her. She responded to me in such a sweet way it took me off guard and encouraged me too. We had text each other on and off for months about schedules and small talk and then that one day she sent me that random text. In her text, Kelly thanked me for showing her the light of Jesus. Her life was now different because she is walking with Jesus every day and boy is He blessing her in many ways!

God wants to use you. Sure, we may have days where we just aren't feeling like stepping out of our comfort zones, but God needs us to be the light. We aren't perfect but we have the perfect Heavenly Father and He will work through us if we allow Him the freedom to do so. With Christ working through us, He will guide us and help us show His love to so many people who truly need Him.

"We're not asking you to be perfect on every play. What we're asking of you and what you should be asking of each other is to give a perfect effort from snap to whistle".

– Coach Bob Ladouceur

Day 30

Be the Wife

Proverbs 18:22, "He who finds a wife finds what is good and receives favor from the Lord."

A good marriage begins in us. Yes, I totally just put it on us as a wife, though I know our husband plays a role, too. We have all heard the phrase, "If mama isn't happy, nobody is happy!" It's easy to allow ourselves to be the happy one at the expense of everyone else's happiness. It makes for a good country song, but it's not the way we should act as Christian women. Before you throw dirt at your husband, look in the mirror and ask God what you might need to change.

I remember when I was cleaning the home of a high ranking family (I performed residential cleaning for over 10 years). I told the wife I loved the way she dressed. What she told me has stuck with me for the past twelve years: "I dress how I want my husband to be respected at work." Maybe you're shaking your head, thinking "I'll dress however I want", but it is great advice. If we are looking out for ourselves alone, how is that helping our husband? I'm not saying to place your identity in your husband because we both know our identity is in the One who made us. We are to be mirrors of God's image. If we are like Christ, we want the best for others, especially our husband.

Think today of something you can do to benefit your husband. Maybe it's simply making dinner or setting up a date night? One day, the kiddos and I wrote sixty or so encouraging notes and Adella even drew pictures on Post-it Notes for Samuel. We drove to his work, snuck in his truck and put them all over the inside of his windows. He was so surprised at the end of the day that he took a selfie with all the notes behind him. He was so happy and felt so loved! It's the little, inexpensive things that mean the most. It's easy to post "woe is me" statuses on social media instead of focusing on how to become our husband's helpmate. Apply God's grace today, and ask Him to strengthen you in this area. It's never too late to become the wife He's called you to be!

"Let the wife make her husband glad to come home and let him make her sorry to see him leave."

-Martin Luther

Day 31

Fall Forward

Philippian's 3:13b-14 "...Forgetting what is behind and straining toward what is ahead, I press on toward the goal to win the prize for which God has called me heavenward in Christ Jesus. "

Do you ever judge yourself at night when you lay in bed? Do you think to yourself, "Did I yell too much today? Should I have bought those jeans? Oh man! I should have called her back? I can't believe I ate that whole bag of donuts!" As women we examine ourselves, and some of us do it to the point where we look in the mirror and make ourselves sick.

I've definitely had my share of those moments. I wish I could say I've lived a sinless life, but I am not perfect. There are many things I want to take back, but I know now those moments have made me a stronger wife, mother, daughter, friend, and woman of God.

When I moved out of my parents' home, I would go to church on Wednesdays and Sundays, but the God I praised on those days of the week was not affiliated in my everyday life. I found myself wasting away spiritually, making poor decisions. When I finally came clean to God, I asked Him to purify me from the inside out. I wanted to be the girl I was at church all the time, totally relaying on Him and Him alone.

After about six months of seeking God, He put on my heart to start writing Samuel, though I didn't care too much for him at the time. We had attended youth group together when we were younger, but at this time in my life, I never saw myself dating him. But God truly put it on my heart to write Samuel a letter of encouragement. My parents jokingly say, "That was some letter of encouragement" because it wasn't even two years later that we were married.

Did I make choices that set me back? Most definitely, but when God sees your brokenness and you repent, He cleanses you. When I fell, I believe I fell forward. I know that same healing can be yours too. Instead of falling backwards, meaning you learned nothing from the sin, you fall forward. When you fall forward, you're still moving in a forward motion. You just need to pick yourself back up and press on.

As the saying goes, your mess becomes your message. You have a powerful message inside of you that can bring a godly change to those around you, people who share the same hurts. The Holy Spirit in you will give you the grace and wisdom to fall forward into the bright future God has always had for you. Trust his leading.

"People fall forward to success"

-Mary Kay Ash

Day 32

Hope

Hebrews 11:1, "Now faith is the substance of things hoped for, the evidence of things not seen.

What is Hope? A feeling or expectation for a certain thing to happen.

Do you know your hope gives faith substance? You can't have faith without hope.

I really enjoy baking for friends and even for the Marines in my husband's shop. One day, I was baking brownies for my husband's work and I started thinking of how my hope gives faith substance. As I grabbed the bowl, I thought the bowl represents me. Every day, I put different things in my bowl, but today is different-- I am really needing God to step in my life for a certain desire or need to be fulfilled. In boxed brownies, you put the oil amount required. The oil represents the Word of God, and it is followed by water, which is your faith. Now, what do water and oil do? They separate. The Word of God doesn't grab on to faith-- it needs faith to make the finished project, but it can't grab on to it yet. You need to rely on the Holy Spirit, which are the eggs in your brownie mix. Your ingredients are in the bowl, but the mix still doesn't look like brownies. You have a bowl, oil, water, and eggs but no substance for any of this to grab on to. What does faith grab on to? Hope, or in this case, brownie mix. Then, after some pressure, heat and time spent with God, your finished project is what you hoped for...a brownie!

You have a power the world around you wants to take from you. You may be hoping for a baby but the doctors are telling you it will never happen. Don't cling to that report! If your desire is to have a baby, God put that desire in you. He will bless you with that baby. Although it may take time for you to hold that baby in your arms, cling to God's hope. His hope is more than wishing upon a star. His hope brings fulfillment. When you are wanting God to do something in your life, if your desires line up with the promises in His word, God said He will give you the desires of your heart, if you ask. Some may tell you that you're out of your mind. It's ok! You're the one with the dream. Not everyone will be excited and motivated by your dream. It's up to you! Raise your hope meter, and make today the day you chose to use your faith unlike ever before!

Psalms 37:4, "Take delight in the Lord, and he will give you the desires of your heart."

Day 33

Reflection

Proverbs 31: 10-12, "A wife of noble character who can find? She is worth far more than rubies. Her husband has full confidence in her and lacks nothing of value. She brings him good not harm, all the days of her life."

Mirror, mirror on the wall who is the most Proverbs 31 women of them all? We sometimes find ourselves reading Proverbs 31, and getting frustrated with this woman. How can one lady have it all together? I mean, come on! She both owns a vineyard and has servant girls to manage? She has so much going on in her life, and she's doing it so well. When I read about her, I find motivation to be on top of my own little world. Being a wife isn't about being perfect, but truly wanting to be more like Christ. When we find ourselves going after the things of Christ, we are not taking up the latest "secret" gossip that's going on around us. Instead, we are finding ways to help our neighbors. Instead of maxing out a store credit card, we are signing up to serve a meal to first time parents.

God has chosen you to be right where you are to help those around you. It's not about taking charge of a vineyard, but taking charge of your Christian walk with Christ. It's about being the light on your street, the home others know they can go to for small group or prayer. God has you right where you are on purpose. He looks at you and says, "Yep, that's my girl! She's shining her light by helping her neighbors by watching their children or fur-baby." Your reflection will radiate Christ.

Every day, we are bombarded with images all around us of fun make up and stylish hair styles. Believe me, I enjoy those things too, but when we find ourselves more into our outward appearance than what is inside, we have a big problem. I tell Adella when she is being feisty, "You can be pretty on the outside, but when you act unsweet to others around you, that can make you seem ugly." When God sees us, He can see our caring and giving heart (or the opposite of those). Let's work on having a beautiful reflection of Him.

Friend, you're greater than you think. We are all a work in progress, and we are all progressing to become a better person. The only competing you should be doing is with who you were yesterday. Focus on becoming more like Christ and becoming the best you.

"As we grow closer to Jesus our lives will reflect Him more clearly."

- Unknown Author

Day 34

Irritations

Luke 6:31, "Do to others as you would have them do to you."

If you have been with your husband for some time, there have probably been many things that irritate you about his job. When you're married to him, it doesn't just irritate you, it forms you. Standing beside my man, I've noticed the irritations to his job have helped form my personality. Before my husband and I were married, I had a plan. I knew where I was going to live the next year and what I would be doing. I was organized and enjoyed routine. What I found out, after marrying my oh-so good looking Marine, was that the plans we made last month would most likely change. That irritated me. I couldn't plan and organize fun things to do! What we don't always realize is that those things that irritate us are actually forming a beautiful life we can share with other women who haven't gone through the same deployment cycle or joys of relocating yet.

Do you know how a pearl is formed? A pearl begins when a foreign substance slips into the oyster between the mantle and the shell which irritates the mantle. The oyster's natural reaction is to cover up that irritant to protect itself, and this eventually forms a pearl. An oyster produces this beautiful gem, and the harvesters then take it out to make a cute necklace. We all can learn from what we have or are currently going through in life. Later on, we can give someone the advice that we learned through that same irritation.

Let God help you whenever you get in an irritating situation. Turn that frustration into someone else's success story. When my husband was attending a Professional Military Education course, we only had one vehicle and his motorcycle. For this course, he needed to wear a nice uniform for a few days, not the typical cammies. He couldn't ride his bike and expect his nice uniform to stay wrinkle free, so I needed to take him to the course. We had one kiddo at the time, I was pregnant and I needed the car throughout the day. It was a little irritating to get up at 4:00 a.m. to take him, but I knew it needed to be done. When you feel yourself becoming irritated, remind yourself of how the pearl is formed. Make your life a constant pearl maker. Take the negative situations life has thrown at you and bless others with advice or even your time. Your life will be such a reflection of Christ when you bless others with help.

"No Grit, No Pearl"

-Unknown Author

Day 35

Walk With Me

Matthew 11:29, "Walk with me and work with me. Watch how I do it. Learn the unforced rhythms of grace. I won't lay anything heavy or ill-filling on you." The Message Bible

God is asking us to walk with him. Who among us can say they have someone with us 24/7 that we completely trust? Only God can be trusted this way. Friend, even as we face hard times with deployment, job changes, missed promotions, and the many different challenges that come with being a military wife, God is asking us to walk with him. He wants us to learn the unforced rhythms of grace. When we think of a spa day (or for the not-so-girlie wives, a night camping under the stars), we think about feeling refreshed. For me, when I typed out both of those outings, I took a deep sigh. I find both of those very peaceful and relaxing. When we read about God's grace, those two things are such little examples compared to His grace. His grace isn't something that is forced on you, like going through a deployment. No, His grace is calm and flows on us without us even having to fight for it. When we are camping, the nights in front of the fire, looking up at the stars are so sweet. In those moments, I wish I could freeze. When we take the peace of a spa day or a camping night, we take in God's grace. God will not force His grace on us, His grace is simply waiting for you to request it. Today, in all the craziness of being a wife, breathe in His grace.

God is promising us He won't allow anything on us that will be heavy. God is saying, "Come, walk with me, and I will make your way straight." When all around you seems to be crashing down, He will raise you up and walk right beside you. God knows how hard it is on us to receive the news our husband is deploying or that we have to uproot the children again from the friends they love. He knows.

Today, trust Him more than you ever have. Walk with Him and He will be right by your side.

Let me pray with you:

Dear God, I ask you to send reminders of love into my friend's life. I pray, Lord, she will feel that you are with her no matter where she goes. Give her the strength and the grace she needs. Thank you for walking with her every day and giving her guidance. We look to you in everything!

In Jesus' name, Amen.

Day 36

Dream a Big Dream

2 Timothy 2:15, "Do your best to present yourself to God as one approved, a worker who does not need to be ashamed and who correctly handles the word of truth."

You have a dream in your heart that was placed there by God. Only you can take the first step and trust that it is God who put that dream there.

What does it take to see your dream fulfilled?

You need to be passionately committed, immoveable. If you're not completely committed to something, your desire may not come to pass. Everyone usually thinks about dieting or working-out when they hear the word "commitment". However, think of your marriage. If you are truly committed to your husband, there's certain things you will do for him. For instance, keeping our house clean (either by us cleaning our homes ourselves or at least having someone else clean it if need be). We could be responsible to make dinner, and fold his clothes for him. The list of ways we can help our husband could go on and on! If you're not committed to him, he will be able to see that in your speech, your actions, and your attitude towards him. The same thing applies to the dream God placed in your heart. If you're not truly committed to it, you won't focus on the things necessary to see it come to pass.

Here are some questions to ask yourself:

What are your goals? Do you have anything written down on paper? What are you doing today to prepare for tomorrow's opportunity?

I know I gave you several questions to consider today. I encourage you to make notes to yourself and look back at them as you get further in this devotional as well anytime in the future. Friend, I really want your dream to be fulfilled. You may be asking me, "Why do you care about my dream when we've never met?" Because if God gave you a dream, I know it's not just for you! It's for so many other people, and you're going to make an impact for eternity. That's why I'm so excited!

"Most people fail, not because of lack of desire, but, lack of commitment."

– Vince Lombardi

Day 37

Push Play

Philippians 3:13, "Forgetting what is behind and straining toward what is ahead."

When we moved to Kaneohe Bay from southern California, we chose to downsize. We owned a home in California and were moving on to base housing which had a slightly smaller floorplan. We could take everything we owned, even the items we really didn't need, but we chose to give them away to make room for the items we did need to live comfortably. When you get new furniture, do you keep the old furniture and add the new furniture to the same space? No! You make room for the new. The same is true in our lives. If we have too much hurt and regret in our hearts and minds, there is no room for God to place His plans and purposes. Stop replaying old discussions, old hurtful emails, and old dirty looks shot your way. Let's push play on the awesome things God has in store for you. Turn some ministry on from encouraging pastors or turn on some good praise tunes. Believe me, reading this is much easier than actually doing it. I know this will take a great deal of prayer and maybe even tears. If you let those things go, God can do amazing things in and through you.

It can be hard to understand that we could be the one holding back the good God has for us. We can hold back the plans God had designed for us since we were little girls. We could be doing this by replaying our past regrets and blaming parents, grandparents, or teachers. As women, it's easy for us to snap back into the past. However, at some point we are going to have to let it go! There are certain things our parents may not have taught us because they were raised in a different generation. Friend, God has such a smoking hot plan for your life, but we need to start letting the bad go and move forward into the good plans God has just for you!

Your past may not look great, but that's ok! It's in your past. Your future looks sweet--- if you can let your past go.

"Until you let your past die your future will never live."

-Jimmy Evans.

Day 38

Keep the Faith

2 Timothy 4:7, "I have fought the good fight, I have finished the race, I have kept the faith."

Deployments are no joke! There isn't anything easy about them. If you don't have children, people say deployment is supposed to be easier, but I remember the struggle of deployment still being hard. After coming home from work, the house was completely quiet--and so unbearable. I remember filling the empty space of our apartment with many tears. The first few days of my husband being away were so hard. I wanted the time we were separated to go by fast so we could be together again. I'd keep my phone glued to my hip, taking it to the bathroom with me to make sure I didn't miss a call. As military spouses, we find the meaning of the word "endurance" through deployments. We know we have to continue on as though nothing is wrong, knowing we will somehow get through this time apart.

When you have children, you don't have the quiet house, but you do have unending questions coming at you: When is dad coming back? Why is he gone again? It feels like when you hit a dry spell of tears and you manage to finally make it one day without crying, another question pops up to remind you it is hard doing this parenting thing alone.

I can get frustrated when my civilian family and friends say, "The time will fly by, just stay busy." I sometimes want to take off my meek badge and say, "No, it won't go by fast! Who are you kidding?!" As frustrating as the comments are, I have to remember they're just trying to comfort me because that's what family and friends do.

With a deep breathe, I tell you this: deployments stink, but God is with you and me during them. After the first three weeks, I usually have a much clearer view that, even though I cry more often than I'd care to admit, God is with me. During times of physical separation with my husband, I stay close to Jesus. Put Him first during deployments. Keep the faith and I promise you, you will feel so thankful after the deployment is over.

Hold on to this: Deuteronomy 31:6, *"Be strong and courageous. Do not be afraid or terrified because of them, for the LORD your God goes with you; he will never leave you nor forsake you."* Put on your cute spiritual shoes and run the race that is before you.

"When we put God first, all other things fall into their proper place or drop out of our lives."

–Ezra Taft Benson

Day 39

Different

Romans 12:2, "Do not conform any longer to the pattern of this world, but be transformed by the renewing of your mind. Then you will be able to test and approve what God's will is--his good, pleasing and perfect will."

You've heard the phrase, "When in Rome, do as the Romans do." Really? Just because we are military wives doesn't mean we need to go spend every penny of the paycheck or make sure the refrigerator is stocked with beer. Come on, we are in the world but we are not of it.

You have to ask yourself...Do you make choices based on what your friends or even what the higher up's wives will think of you. If your quiet answer is yes, then today is the perfect day to change!

God has called you to do so much more than average living. Just because TV shows portray military wives as "hoochies" while their husband is away doesn't mean that has to be you. Dr. Seuss has asked each of us a very profound question,

"Why fit in when you were born to stand out?" Going with the flow can lead to the destruction of a marriage or your self-worth.

You are chosen for such a time as this. With all that is going on in the world around us, we need to receive courage from God and be the light instead of going with the norm.

The story of Esther is so special. At first, Esther didn't want to step out and be different. It looked dangerous—she could possibly lose her life as well as the lives of her people, the Jews. Nevertheless, Esther followed the leading of her godly Uncle Mordecai and of the Holy Spirit (Esther 1-9). You think being a military wife isn't dangerous? It may not be as intense as Esther's life, but there will be days when it seems like too much. Car pools can get pretty intense-- even dinner time for that matter-- and I don't know about you, but doing homework with your child may make you want to pull your hair out (especially if your child tells you, "that's not the way my teacher does it.").

Ladies, I'm telling you, you were born for this! You were singled out by God to be your husband's wife, and he needs you to be healthy and full of encouragement. You are amazing! You have what it takes! Keep going after the things of God and run your race!

"It takes nothing to join the crowd. It takes everything to stand alone."

–Hans F. Hansen

Day 40

You're Chosen!

Matthew 22: 14, "For many are called, but few are chosen."

You have been chosen and appointed to become a military wife. There is no one who can do it better than you for your husband. God has already given you the strength you need to be the perfect helper for him. Whether he is getting ready to deploy or working from sun up until sun down. You are there to help him stay focused on his job and to help him remember that his home life matters. Some of our husbands get so caught up in their work that they may need you to lovingly remind him to make time to call his parents or to send gifts to his family members for their birthdays and holidays.

For our spouse, being at work and being at home are two very different worlds. Similar to most occupations, there are constant pressures and influences from this world he is constantly fed and exposed to. He is being bombarded with worldly ways, thoughts, and lifestyles. From the not so great language used in the squadron, to the images other guys look at on their personal devices. Your husband needs your help more than you may realize. Whether he tells you or not, he depends on you to build a calming and peaceful home environment for your family. He needs your help to monitor media consumption, your children's friends, and the kinds of social gatherings that take place in your home.

Your responsibility as a military wife may seem overwhelming at times, but don't give into anxiety (see Isaiah 35:4 and Matt 6:25-34). You will be tempted to give up--don't! You have to remember the Greater One is in you. You have the ability inside of you to be the ultimate military wife. Not because of our own strength. You and I don't have it. Only God has the strength and He will carry us through it all if we will keep choosing to press on.

One afternoon I received a text message from a friend of mine in distress who happened to be fighting the same battles while her husband was deployed. Her text read: "Is this worth it? I am tired of being alone at night and having the kids suffer with not having daddy around. Is this worth it?" I lay there for a few minutes, alone in my big king size bed, pondering the question. Finally I had to shake myself out of it. Looking over at his empty pillow I said to myself "Yes this is worth it!" We, as military wives, all have nights when we are just so sad that he isn't with us. We all have those nights when the pillow is soaked with tears. Believe me. I get it. I quickly sent a text message back to my sweet friend saying "You know it's worth it."

Friend, I know the nights can be lonely and the days can seem forever since we last heard from our loved ones. Is it worth it? Yes, it's worth staying pure and keeping the faith. You, my friend, can do this! Will it be easy? Not a chance, but I promise you God will see you through all the uncertainties of this military life. Be there for your husband and encourage him when the situation seems hopeless. You got this girl because God has you!

"Don't allow yourself to think your life is insignificant. You are God's very handiwork. Chosen and commissioned for His purposes!

-Charlotte Gambill

Day 41

The Sparrow

Matthew 10:29, 31, "Are not two sparrows sold for a penny? Yet not one of them will fall to the ground outside your Father's care. So don't be afraid; you are worth more than many sparrows."

On day two after my husband had left home on his second MEU deployment, the kiddos and I were all still feeling very sad by his absence. We had the opportunity to have a fun beach day with friends from out of state the day prior, and on this particular day I needed to make curtains for a room due to my parents planning to visit with us. As I was going through my sewing box, I stumbled upon a brooch in the shape of a sparrow (like what you would wear pinned to a shirt). I had never seen this pin before and I have had my sewing box since I was probably ten years old. When I saw that pin I lost it, tears streamed down my face. My husband had been away so much within the four previous years from the work-ups, training and deployments. When I saw that pin I knew God was reminding me He. Has. Me.

Deployments are so hard, but God is truly with us. He. Has. You. Too. No matter what may come and no matter the situation, God is truly watching over us.

After seeing the sparrow pin and just sensing God's presence, I knew He wasn't just reminding me, He wanted you to know that as well, He has you. When Deployments, training exercises and work ups come, it's going to be challenging. Something will break or malfunction. The first few weeks take some adjusting as we make a new routine, but if we to go to God each day, He will keep reminding us that He is with us. God never wants us to feel alone. If you go to God each day and ask Him to be with you and give you peace of mind, He will do just that. During the MEU deployment, so much was on the news about the MEU my husband was on. Every time I looked at the news feeds through my smartphone, it seemed like "There's his ship again." It was hard to see and hear what the news reporters were saying, but I just had to trust God that just like He has me and my children, He has my husband too. God is with us friend, He sees how badly it hurts us when our spouse is away. Remember today, He has you and you are so valuable to Him, you and your family.

"His eyes are on the sparrow and I know He watches over me."

-Civilla D. Martin

Day 42

Boundaries

Matthew 26:41, "Watch and pray so that you will not fall into temptation. The spirit is willing, but the flesh is weak."

Many of us have boundaries we have placed on ourselves in our minds. For example...As a married woman, I would never text a picture of myself to another guy. This is a pretty normal boundary to have as a married woman. Honestly, though, Christian women need to step it up a notch.

What might cause you to fall? It always starts with the littlest things. You don't just start sleeping with another man. It could start "just" by seeing how that ex-boyfriend from high school is doing...you "just" try to friend him on Facebook.

When my husband left for Iraq, I was working as a receptionist. One of the employees was a single guy. He told me almost every day he liked my outfit, which was weird seeing how he wasn't my husband. I said thank you and continued on with my day. As an avid coffee drinker, every day I brought in a coffee with me to work. One day after our lunch break this young man came into my office acting all proud of himself. Behind his back, he had my favorite coffee and a gift card to my favorite coffee shop. He said, "I wanted to get you this to tell you what a great job you're doing here." I honestly didn't see this coming. I felt very strange when he did that for me. Needless to say, I put in my two week notice. I worked as a church receptionist, but working in a church doesn't mean you can't be tempted. While I hadn't been tempted to that point, I knew that young man had been tempted. I'm not saying to quit your job every time someone is flirting with you. In my case, I knew it was best. In your case, talking with your manager and seeing how the company can help may be more appropriate.

You have to really examine the situation, especially if a guy other than your husband is texting you nice little things such as, "You're so amazing" or "Wow! You brighten my day." We have to be cautious! Begin to pray that God will help you be wise and not naive. Being naive may be cute, but it can lead to destruction. God will show us what boundaries need to have set in place and He will give us the grace to stay within them.

Hosea 4:6, "My people are destroyed from lack of knowledge...."

Day 43

Temptation

1 Corinthians 10:13, "No temptation has overtaken you except what is common to mankind. And God is faithful; he will not let you be tempted beyond what you can bear. But when you are tempted, he will also provide a way out so that you can endure it."

As military wives, there are so many temptations that come our way. Wouldn't you agree? Let me give you some examples. Fear can creep in as you're waiting for moving orders. The temptation of adultery can creep in when a nice guy asks you to the movies to "lift your spirits." The temptation to compare comes in when you see the perfectly airbrushed women in magazines.

Many temptations, as difficult as they may seem, can be conquered by staying focused on your time with God. If you indulge yourself in God's Word and make Him your first priority, God will provide a way of escape when temptation comes. When my husband was deployed for the second time, it seemed like everything went wrong for me. Some people have labeled facing crisis during a deployment as a "deployment curse." You see, you're not alone. Bad things happen, and this may seem especially true when your husband is away. When Sam was deployed, I had to find a new job because the family I was a nanny for was moving away. I had no friends because we had recently moved to a new area. To top it off, I found out I was pregnant with our first child. Being pregnant was a blessing, but the timing didn't feel all that great. I was smacked in the face with the temptation to freak out and fear, but God came to my rescue. In devotion time, He truly showed me I needed to completely rely on Him, so I did. Everything worked out—I even found the perfect job.

God is there for you. Seek Him first. When you do and you're confronted with a temptation, God will show you a way of escape. I know you'll feel Him with you each step of the way.

"If we do not abide in prayer, we abide in temptation."

-John Owen

Day 44

Feelings

Proverbs 28:26, "Those who trust in themselves are fools, but those who walk in wisdom are kept safe."

On Christmas break of 2015, my family and I took a two week vacation to visit family out of state. The morning of the first day back to school, I was waking Elijah when he said, "I don't feel like going to school today. Why can't it just be summer break?!" Isn't it so easy, even for us adults, to make choices based on our feelings? Would we ever choose responsibility over fun?

God doesn't want us to be controlled by our feelings. Feelings are simply an emotional state. I don't know about you, but every month during a specific time I seem to get a real "fog" going on. Instead of being controlled by the Holy Spirit I have often allowed myself to be controlled by my emotional, un-balanced hormones. Studies have shown women act different while they are on their monthly cycle. I recently had an encounter with God and He revealed to me I was in the wrong when I allowed myself to be controlled by my feelings, even when it's a chemical thing. Yes, it's very challenging to control my feelings during "that time of the month," but emotions can be controlled. They cannot be controlled by you on your own, but by the Holy Spirit in you. You have to rely on Him, especially when the enemy distracts you during that special time of the month. Don't allow your head to be filled with all kinds of negativity and sadness. You need to come at the enemy with the Word just like Jesus did when he was tempted. You can come at the enemy by saying, I am a child of the most High God. I am not controlled by my feelings-- I am controlled by the Holy Spirit. At times, you will want to justify yourself and let nature have its way, but you shouldn't. When the cycle is complete, you will have regrets. Wouldn't you rather look back at yourself and say, "Sure, I became a little bloated, but my mind and my actions were controlled. God was able to use me to be an encourager to someone else." By allowing the precious Holy Spirit to be your controller, you will surprise yourself. You will get through that time and praise God for giving you everything you needed to overcome.

"Feelings are much like waves, we can't stop them from coming but we can choose which one to ride."

-Unknown Author

Day 45

A New Mindset

1 Thessalonians 5:21, "but test them all; hold on to what is good."

I was never a runner when I was younger. I played recreational and travel soccer, but I never considered myself an athlete. When my coaches wanted us to run I would always be the last one back. When I became a mom of two, I decided I wanted to start working out again. My husband encouraged me to start running with him (May I remind you he is a Marine. Marines can be intense when it comes to running!). When he first brought the idea up to me, I thought he was a little crazy. He knew I didn't like running, that I was more of a work out video gal. Well, I eventually let him talk me into it. I even bought a jogging stroller off Craigslist so we wouldn't be held back by the kids. My husband pushed me until I thought I was going to die. Honestly, I thought I was going to throw up every time--I even cried a few times (Seriously!). My husband wouldn't let me quit. He was and is still my motivator to this day. Because everything in the military must eventually change, my husband eventually had to go back to working long hours which prevented us from carrying on our jogging routine together. I knew when that happened I was going to need to continue to run all by myself if I was going to continue improving my overall health. I was pleasantly surprised that I got to the point where if I didn't run, I found I missed doing it. It felt so great to go on a run. I'm able to look back at those first months and I know there is no way I was running on my own strength--- it was all God power.

With running, the first thing I had to do was to change my mind about it. I had to make the decision myself. My husband couldn't change my mind about it--- I had to be the one to make the change; to choose to change.

It's the same way in our Christian walk. We have to be the one to choose to make the changes in our own life. Having Faith is a choice. If we allow doubt to creep in, it cripples our faith and what faith can do in our life. We won't be able to clearly see the change we need to make or have the full power of the Holy Spirit working through us. Part of that power comes from knowing the Word. It's one thing to memorize scriptures, but if you're not putting the scriptures to use, the words in the Bible are only words. You have to believe the Word is more than beautiful words. It contains powerful and life-changing words.

When we choose Jesus Christ, He is life-changing. Nothing about our life will be ordinary.

Mighty woman of God, He has you and His love for you is beyond anything you could dream. He puts no pressure on you. He asks you to put the pressure on His words. We need to make those words jump off the pages and into our daily life by choosing to have faith in very one who spoke those words, allowing them to change us.

"Every thought we think is creating our future."

–Louise Hay

Day 46

Tradition

Colossians 1:17, "And he is before all things, and in him all things hold together."

Every branch of the military has its own set of traditions. Some are really fun like the Marine Corps Ball because you can get dressed up. Others can make you shake your head—like the geedunk (you'll have to ask your husband about that one).

As you go throughout this week, think about the traditions you have in your home. For instance, is it a tradition in your home to pray before you eat? It's the small traditions that will make a big impact on your children's future and the future of your marriage. Traditions can set you and your family up for beautiful moments and memories, but if you allow the small traditions like praying for your food get swept away, what are your children's traditions going to be when they are grown?

In our house, our Christmas tradition is to read the Christmas story about Jesus' birthday before opening presents. Growing up, it's something my parents did on Christmas morning and I thought it was something to pass on to my children. Traditions both good and bad can be passed on without us even realizing. My parents didn't know that I would grab on to that tradition, but they instilled it in me none the less.

One tradition that can cause damage to your soul is nagging. Nagging causes things to come out of your mouth that you don't even mean to say. It causes your actions to be something out of a scary movie. I had one of those scary moments when I found myself nagging my husband. After nagging him, I went into another room and immediately felt so bad. I could feel God speaking to my heart about how this is a common action of mine when my husband pushes my buttons. I asked God to forgive me and to help me to change. I went back to my husband and apologized for my behavior. He simply smiled and said, "It's okay, babe." Jesus holds our marriage together, but only if we seek Him and have him be at center of our family. God is there for you, too. He wants to help you make good traditions in your home. If you weren't raised in a home where Jesus was the center and you have traditions in your home that are ungodly, that's okay. God will give you fresh ideas on how to tear down those habits or traditions and re-center your life around Him. He will either place ideas in your mind or He will place Godly believers in your life to help you see how to bring Christ into your home to start traditions of your own. God is just so amazing like that. He wants to see you thrive! Matthew 6:23 says "But seek first the kingdom of God and his righteousness, and all these things will be added to you."

"At the heart of every family tradition is a meaningful experience."

—Unknown Author

Day 47

Empower

Proverbs 18:21a, "The tongue can bring death or life..."

Have you ever had a really down moment? I was having one of those moments when my husband was away on a deployment. That moment changed, however; when my sweet friend texted me some encouraging quotes. In that moment, she was empowering me to move forward with a smile on my face.

Our words speak power over someone. Our words will make or break our marriage. Our words will make or break the way our children see themselves and the world around them.

We've all heard the boot camp stories and seen the emotion expressed by the one sharing the story. In Quantico, Virginia there is a museum called, The National Marine Corps Museum. At the boot camp exhibit, there are yellow footprints for the visitors to follow. Spoiler alert: as soon as your feet touch those footprints, you are blown away by the recording of a drill instructor yelling at you. Now think of your home. Is the atmosphere thick with hurt from words that were spoken? Words can affect your whole day—even your whole life! The men and women who choose to go through boot camp know it won't be easy, but they push through. I can't help but think about our homes. Do we really want to feel like we have to push through each day?

It's challenging enough outside the home where people often don't get along, but having to push through each day while in the security of your own home could get overwhelming. Ask God to help you with your words to be slow to speak and quick to listen.

You were put on this earth; you were put on that base you live in; your place of employment; or even the school you're attending so that you can reach out to others. Let's speak life and empower those around us, especially our husband and our children. Let your children know they built that toy car great or put their shoes on really good. Our families need sweet words dropped into them that will change their day for the better.

"A wise woman knows the importance of speaking life into her man. If you love him: believe in him, encourage him and be his peace."-Denzel Washington

Day 48

Standing Strong

Hebrews 10:23, "Let us hold unswervingly to the hope we profess, for he who promised is faithful."

Do your children ever tell you their feet hurt or your husband comes home after a long day's work and tells you how sore his feet are? Standing can be tough, especially when we don't know how long we will be standing for. As you can tell, I'm not just talking about the regular standing, I'm talking about standing through all life's challenges.

We have to ask ourselves: Will we trust in God when times are troubling? We can talk all we want in church how "God's got this". However, when the paycheck runs out, you have a really bad toothache, and to top it all off you're moving from Hawaii to North Carolina, life can be tough. Yes, as descriptive as all that sounds (and probably a little funny) that was my story from our PCS in 2015. I had to ask myself that same question. Will I trust God even though all of this is going on? Yes, even though thoughts come in those times as if saying, "You won't make it this time in this situation. This problem is much worse than the other times". In these moments I have to quickly remind myself God has never failed me, not once; and there is no way He will start failing me now. God is such a good Father (Read Hebrews 13:5).

When our husband is standing at attention, he knows there is an important moment about to take place and he is ready to show honor and respect. In the same way when we are standing on God's promise during challenging times, God sees we are not giving into the temptation or into fear. He sees us putting all our hope in Him and He takes action. Standing on His promises will never fail us (Read Isaiah 55:11).

Be on guard. It's easy to get discouraged when you're trying to stand strong. Remember that God is faithful. When we stand on His promises and keep our trust in Him no matter what the News is saying about the whereabouts of our husband's unit or what the negative doctor report is, if we keep standing in His promise of what His words say regarding His protection and healing (Psalms 91:7 & James 5:15), we will see the promise we are standing on be fulfilled.

"We can't and we should not, compare suffering. We come together as a family of God, hand in hand. And then together coming and standing upon the promises of

God, knowing that no matter who you are, no matter what you're going through,

that God knows it, He is with you, He is going to pull you through."

–Nick Vujicic

Day 49

Removing the Labels

John 8:36, "So, if the Son sets you free, you will be free indeed."

When I was in Elementary and Middle School I had teachers that labeled me dyslexic. For some reason I just was not good at reading. Books that you would think a fifth grader could breeze right through, I would have the hardest time with, (i.e. Clifford the Big Red Dog by Norman Bridwell). I would completely stumble through those books. One time, I had a teacher blatantly call me to the front of the classroom to show my weakness to everyone in the room by having me read aloud from the dictionary. I was so humiliated I put the book down and ran out of class. I was completely embarrassed and frustrated with myself.

Unfortunately, I know I am not alone with reading frustrations. It wasn't until my husband and I started doing devotions together as adults that God completely did a work in me. My husband really encouraged me to do the Bible reading portion and he would end it by saying the prayer. I owe it all to God. I was finally able to shake off the label others had put on me and became confident, not in my ability to read, but in God's ability to help me.

The first time I had to read in front of a large group of people later on, I was still a little nervous, but I knew I had to stop putting my faith in myself and start putting my faith fully on Christ. He gave me the confidence to remove the label others had put on me and that I had accepted for myself. It's our act of faith that releases us from the labels that are stuck on us given from others or that we have put on ourselves like, "I'll never be good enough".

Let's make a fresh start today and remove the labels, whatever they may be; not educated enough, not healthy enough, the list could keep going with all the labels that are put on people. We need to remind our self of who we are in Christ; beautiful, accepted and graced for your family that you're raising and the husband that you have. Labels could be the only thing holding you back from the amazing plan God designed for you from before you were even born. Remove the labels today and except the plan God has for you.

Let me pray for you:

Dear God, I pray for my friend, that she will be able to identify the labels that have been put on her by others or even herself. Help her to lay all the labels down before you. Help her to find confidence in you and what you call her; blessed and beautiful.

In Jesus' name, Amen.

Day 50

With Much Delight

Psalm 73:25, "... And earth has nothing I desire besides you."

To delight means happiness or to show pleasure in something. When we are wanting more of the same things that God is wanting for our life rather than desiring to have the best looking house on the block or other material things, than we can't say we are desiring God's plan over our own. I'm not saying God doesn't want you to have those things or other blessings, but I am saying when we put God first (His plans in His timing) then all those other things will fall into the perfect place for us (Psalms 37:4).

When we were stationed in California we were really wanting to find a church that offered a lot for our children. We had confidence that in praying and asking God to show us where to go that He would place in us the perfect spot just for them. When I saw a church ad online, the church looked so fun and full of activates perfect for our children's ages. The only thing was the drive, the church was a little over an hour away from our home on base. My husband and I said we would go and see if it was really where God wanted us to be. After attending one service, we knew that church was the place for our family. We committed to attending the church Sunday mornings and Wednesday evenings. We knew it was going to be a drive, but we felt so strongly that's where God needed us. We eventually found our delight in His plan, despite the long drive. After 6 months of attending the church, God opened up a door for us to buy a home, and wouldn't you know it, in all the areas God could have opened up a home for us in southern California, the home he blessed us with was only 5 minutes from the church. When we are delighting in God, I know from experience that He opens up doors for you that leave people around you stumped as to how that could ever happen.

Let's choose that no matter what is going on around us, we delight in Him first. Just you wait and see, He has some pretty amazing plans for you and your family, plans to prosper you and not to harm you (Jeremiah 29:11). When we delight in Him, He can show up in some pretty surprising ways.

"Being happy in God is the way we glorify Him. This is the reason we were created. Delighting in God is not a mere performance or option of life; it is our joyful duty and should be the single passion of our lives."

–John Piper

Day 51

Bloom

Psalms 92:13, "Those who are planted in the house of the Lord shall flourish in the courts of our God."

I feel as military spouses we often hear the phrase, "bloom where you're planted." I even bought myself a little garden flag with that phrase on it. After our third big move, I didn't care to put out the flag that I once thought was so cute. Moving can be fun, and yes it is truly an adventure every time that we move.

I was out on a run when God had me look around, I felt him drop this question into my heart: Am I allowing where I live hold me back? For a moment I was confused, I had become so comfortable with where I was at. My husband and I had opened a life group up in our home, we served weekly in our church, and we both felt good about where we were at. Than the orders came in to move again and I could feel myself becoming sad. I was comfortable with my surroundings. My children were even in a wonderful school. I didn't understand why God was asking me that question at this time, I mean we were doing His work, we were serving and truly blooming in our walk and personal life. I didn't understand why God would ask me that question. I thought, I'm a military spouse who never gets to make the decision where we move. I asked God, "Where I'm living hold me back?! God, I didn't want to move here in the first place, and now that I'm comfortable, truly planted, now I already have to be uprooted again?" (I'm sure you are laughing at that remark.)

After I had my little venting session with God He simply reminded me that He will always be with me, He is everywhere. Every day I truly have to trust Him at His words when He said that He would never leave me or forsake me. God has each of us, through the moves, through it all. I had to remind myself, just like gardeners dig up their flowers to allow someone else to enjoy the beauty from them, we too can be just like those flowers. Instead of us getting grumpy and out of sorts, we can picture ourselves as those flowers. The flowers that are much too beautiful to stay in one garden, but are purposed to be shared with so many other people. We know our beauty is because God is in us and His light is in us, so we must find a way to be positive through each uprooting.

Colossians 2:7a, "Plant your roots in Christ and let Him be the foundation for your life." The Contemporary English Version

Day 52

Hard Times Call for Great Faith

Isaiah 43:2, "When you pass through the waters, I will be with you; and when you pass through the rivers, they will not sweep over you. When you walk through the fire, you will not be burned; the flames will not set you ablaze."

Life can be hard but our faith in Christ can stand through the hardest times.

There are going to be moments in your life that are challenging; a deployment, childbirth, a vacation with family members you haven't seen in years, a new job, or maybe your husband changes his career path. Through those challenging times you can either make the choice to walk through it alone and without God's help, or with God's help. By you believing God can get you through the challenge in front of you, you are using your faith.

When we were stationed in Hawaii, I had a sweet friend whose husband put in a package that included a promotion for which he was accepted. The promotion would mean great things for her husband's career and, expectedly, their finances. My friend was a little nervous. She was excited for her husband, but she had heard there were a lot more responsibilities required from them both. These responsibilities included: participation in social events as well as being her husband's helpmate responsible for reaching out to any family members the member may have left behind during a deployment. My friend knew the only way to make this big transition in her life would be going to God for guidance. She once told me, "I found so much peace when I used my faith to get through the first year of the transition. God was truly with me."

Times can get so hard where you can actually see yourself going through them and even questioning yourself: How am I doing this? You must keep pushing through the fear knowing God is still by your side to give you the peace and grace you need to keep going. God loves you so much. He sees all the crazy hard times you are going through. If you keep going and don't give into doubt, you will come out rejoicing in the end with arms up high saying, "I did it" (Galatians 6:9). Just like my friend, you will find peace when you use your faith to keep you going through the hard times.

"Difficult roads often lead to beautiful destinations."

−TobyMac

Day 53

I See You

2 Timothy 2:15, "Do your best to present yourself to God as one approved, a worker who does not need to be ashamed and who correctly handles the word of truth."

I was recently frustrated while attempting to make a return at a local department store. The reason the representative was giving me for rejecting my return didn't make sense to me. At one point I asked myself, would I want my pastor to see me acting like this if he was with me? I immediately got a check in my spirit. I felt God say, "I'm with you always." If you could have saw my reaction as I was right there at the counter you would have seen it hit me. That was a very big moment in my life. Yes, I knew God was always with me, but when I thought about it in that moment a light went off. Sometimes we are more worried about what others on this earth are thinking about us instead of what our heavenly father is seeing from us, and He is the one who determines where we are going to be for eternity.

When my husband and I were first married, he wasn't at the bottom of the barrel when it came to rank, but he was pretty close. I remember countless nights he had to stay late to figure out an aircraft problem. He always held his head so high, even under the frustrations that can arise when you are just learning your job. One day he came home with a broken front tooth and a bruised eye. While working on an aircraft earlier in the day, he was pulling too hard with some pliers while performing some maintenance. The pliers slipped off his job and into his face, breaking his front tooth awkwardly in half. He looked like a hockey player after being hit in the face with a puck. My husband still went to work the next day ready to continue work as usual. He was motivated to keep learning his job. At one point he was given the nickname "Golden boy" by his peers because of all his efforts. He seemed to gain the full confidence of his superiors. You see, when you are someone of character you stay committed no matter what, you give your best and then some. God can only bless you when you put your best attitude into each task you are given.

When we are by ourselves, or with just our children, we have to ask ourselves who we are when no one is looking. To be a women of great character, that's not something we can accomplish overnight. Each morning we have to go to God and ask Him to help us be the wife He needs us to be, the woman He needs us to be. The more we ask God to help shape our character, the closer we are to becoming more like Him. Everyday God is with us. When I was at the local department store, I had to remember that I may be the only Christian someone will meet. How is my character showing them Jesus?

"They'll know we are Christians by our love."

—Peter Scholtes

Day 54

Anchored to Hope

Hebrews 6:19a "We have this hope as an anchor for the soul, firm and secure."

When Samuel was away on his third deployment, I kept hearing others around me say, "I hope he makes it back safely." I would get a little sad because that phrase just seemed so down. It wasn't until I heard a teaching on hope that my apprehension made sense. The pastor said, "You can't have faith without hope". Hope in the Lord is much different from worldly hope. God's hope is true and full of faith.

When we think of hope, sometimes we think of something that could happen, but hope is an action word.

What are you hoping for? Are you wanting a baby but the doctors have told you to give up? A friend of mine at our church in California, Mary, was having problems conceiving a baby. She and her husband wanted a baby so badly, and they were heartbroken after a miscarriage. Mary's passion to keep her faith for a baby was so amazing. One night after church, Mary made a point to come to my car and said,

"Katherine, I'm pregnant!" She was so excited about the awesome news. She told me one thing I will never forget. She said, "Work the Word and the Word will work for you." What did she mean by that? It's one thing to memorize scriptures, but if you're not putting the scriptures to use, the words in the Bible are just that: words. You need to make them work in your life, and that means you have to believe the Word of God. You have to know the Bible doesn't simply contain wonderful words—it contains powerful and life changing words like ammunition for a gun, or.... wait for it.... like a sword. By itself, it is a dangerous weapon, but it will just be sitting there. It can accomplish so much more when you carry the word in your heart and direct it at your targets by both hearing it and speaking it.

When the captain of a ship wants to stay in one place, he puts down the anchor. Even if others on the ship don't think they should stay there, the captain will know if it's the right place for them, and he doesn't move the anchor until he is ready. You need to be like that captain. Even if your friends don't agree with you, don't move your anchor of hope until what you're believing for comes to pass --- no matter the wave. When you factor Jesus into your hopes, He'll bring your hopes to pass. God has you, mighty woman of God, and His love for you is beyond anything you could possible think.

"When darkness seems to hide His face, I rest on His unchanging grace. In every high and stormy gale, my anchor holds within the veil. ...When all around my soul gives way, He then is all my Hope and Stay."

—Hillsong United

Day 55

Listen to the Call

John 10:3a, 5, "... He calls his own sheep by name and leads them out. When he has brought out all his own, he goes on ahead of them, and his sheep follow him because they know his voice..."

When my husband calls me when he is deployed, I get so excited when I hear his voice through the phone. An instant smile appears, no matter what craziness is going on at our house. When he calls me everything stops. All of my attention is his. This last deployment we were only able to talk twice over a two month period, lasting about twenty minutes a call. Isn't it funny how we take our phone with us everywhere, just in case our husband calls? (The toilet paper rack in my restroom has become a great cell phone holder during those months).

After one of the phone calls from my husband, I was reminded of the Bible story of when the prophet Samuel heard from God. In the story it took Samuel a few times to actually know it was God's voice calling to him (1 Samuel 3). Can you think of a time when you thought you heard from God but didn't really respond? Hopefully not out of disobedience, but just out of not really knowing it was God's voice talking to you. I have had those moments when I was a little unsure. One time I really felt God telling me to join someone at the altar to pray with them during worship at our church. I didn't know her or what she might be going through. I was a little like, "Is this God or did I have too many cups of coffee this morning?" The feeling was very strong and I chose to listen. I moved out of my seat and went up to her to ask if I could pray with her. She began to weep and said "Yes. Please do." I was a little nervous about the situation as I went to pray with her. Words came out that really made no sense to me, but she told me that what I prayed for was exactly what she needed. The woman ended up giving her heart to Christ that day with me.

God speaks to each of us every day. It's not that He whispers where it is hard to hear, but sometimes we just get too busy with everyday stuff that we don't really practice listening. God needs you. He needs you to come to Him each day and say, "I am here God, use me." When you open your day to Him, be ready and He will speak to you. Whatever He has called you to do is beyond wonderful!

"The quieter you become, the more you can hear."

–Unknown Author

Day 56

Godly Wisdom

Proverbs 9:10a, "The fear of the Lord is the beginning of wisdom..."

When my husband and I have devotion time in the morning, we pray that God will give us wisdom beyond our years. I know my husband has definitely been blessed with wisdom beyond his years at his job. Things often seem to line up for him so smoothly, we know it's only because of God's hand in our lives guiding us. My husband has worked on aircraft since before we were married. There have been times when people in other countries working on similar helicopters have called upon him to either help them through problems or to even write procedures to be included in maintenance manuals for his particular aircraft. My husband has received the same training as all the other Marines, but I really think something happens in the spirit when we ask God for wisdom. God releases wisdom and allows us to become wiser and to show us things even before they are to happen. King Solomon in the Bible was given Godly wisdom, wisdom beyond his years just by asking God for it (1Kings 3:5-12).

The military is full of packing in training for career progression. There are very skilled teachers that can help our husband learn how to work through complex issues, but when you invite God to come in and add His wisdom to those same decisions, wow! Godly wisdom will amplify the already great training we have received. As wives, and especially for those stay-at-home mommies, we too need a high level of wisdom. Maybe even more so because we are raising children to become Godly adults. There is a lot of pressure on us moms when we are the only parent at home. I honestly can say there isn't a day that goes by where I am not coming to God for wisdom concerning a household issue. God will freely give us the wisdom we need for all our issues, the big and the small.

Did you know you can be very knowledgeable with your education, but that earthly knowledge is not the same as having Godly wisdom? Knowledge is fantastic, but Godly wisdom is far greater (Proverbs 16:16). Our Pastor in North Carolina has said, "Godly wisdom is seeing and responding to life situations with a Godly perspective". You see, even the world around us will tell us we need to go ask a counselor. Everyone we know on our social media accounts seem to have it all figured out and is full of advice. Go to God as your counselor first. Ask God today for the wisdom you are needing in your present situation. When you go to God, He will bless you with the wisdom you need to see the situation and solution more clearly (James 1:5).

"Earthly wisdom is doing what comes naturally. Godly wisdom is doing what the Holy Spirit compels us to do."

-Charles Stanley

Day 57

After the Storm

Psalms 107:29, "He calmed the storm to a whisper and stilled the waves."

Did you know that after a storm there is always a new beginning? It's could be a beginning you never thought would happen, a beginning to something that could be awesome.

After my husband finished one of his training sessions away from home and we were all back together as a family, I looked back over the "storm" that I had felt while he was away. It had been a period that was very hard on me spiritually. My husband said the training was challenging and physically exhausting to him too, but for me it was mostly an exhausting spiritual battle. Apparently, I hadn't been the only one to go through the battle either. I heard reports of other military wives going as far as getting divorced during their husband's absence. During those months I clung to God with all I had, praying every chance I had. I would listen to ministry online just to soak up testimonies of people overcoming huge obstacles. When I looked back over the time we were away from each other and how I connected with God, I know that through the storm my ability to trust in God always increased.

When you get out of the storm, always remember to look back over how you reacted and responded to different things you went through during the storm. As much as we don't like to experience them, remembering what we learned through our storms by recognizing how we responded, and sharing it with those around us can lead someone else through their storm more easily. We have to share with others about the storms that we went through and how God brought us through. It builds our confidence and faith.

I would love to tell you there will be no more storms in your life, but it sometimes seems that the storms get louder as our faith grows stronger. They seem to involve and touch more and more people around us with each new storm, but don't you think that is exactly the plan? That way, as our faith grows more people are able to see God at work and how faithful he will be to each and every one of us.

Try to remember a storm that you went through in the past and how God brought you through. Share it with a friend face-to-face, write it as an encouragement letter to someone you know, or maybe post-it to social media. When we talk about our storms and how we were brought through with God's help, you are worshipping God by reminding others of the good things He has done and is capable of doing.

In that, we are praising God and giving Him the credit. When you come to another storm, remember the same strength and grace you had in the last storm. Press through and know you can come through this one too. You are a fighter of faith. You can overcome any obstacle with the wisdom God has given you. Also, when the waves seem too high, having a leader at your church pray and agree with you, someone you trust and know will pray faith words over your situation, is an excellent source of encouragement.

"When you let God into your life, the storms of life may rise but you will not be shaken."

- John Hagee Ministries

Day 58

Apply Grace

Isaiah 14: 27a, "For the Lord of All has planned, and who can keep it from happening?"

My sweet friend had just received Christ into her heart. She texted me one day and said, "I keep praying God will give me patience in waiting for the next step to take in my life, but I just keep on going through things that I feel are messing it up."

If you're saying the same thing today, I totally understand where you are coming from, but let me say this, friend; when we pray for something like patience, God will test us in our growth. How do you receive a test in patience? Well, God will allow something to show up in your life that will allow you to have to practice your patience. Think of it this way, in school when a teacher is trying to teach you about addition, you first read about it. To start learning about patience, we can read in the Bible about men and women who also experienced the need for patience. A good example is the woman with the issue of blood (Luke 8:40-56). She had to practice patience in finding health through many years and treatments. What happens next in school after your teacher explains it and wants you to really get something? You are tested on that knowledge by applying it to a problem. When you ask God to make you more patient, you are going to be tested in that area. Instead, I suggest we pray God will give us the grace we need for the day. When we have God's grace, there is nothing we will not be able to handle (2 Corinthians 12:8-9). God's grace is a free gift to you. All you need to do is ask for it.

Take on today by applying God's grace to your situation.

Can't find a job? God's grace

PCS'ing? God's grace

Negative doctor report? God's grace

Child misbehaving? God's grace

Feeling stuck? God's grace

When you ask God for His grace in any situation, He will move on your behalf. He will make things that are unknown, known to us. Patience will come, but it will only come when we are focusing on Him. The more we focus on what's not happening or what we are not understanding, the more we get frustrated. When we are relying on God's grace in the situation, that's when we will see change.

In all things apply His grace. When you catch yourself saying to the problem, "I'm done with it, I just can't do anything." God says, "Yes! She's finally ready to ask for my help." He's not waiting for you to fail. He's waiting on you to do it with His strength, not yours.

"God has a purpose for your life. He's already planned out your days. When you're on detour, don't get upset, don't live frustrated, it's one scene. When it all comes together, it's going to work out for your good."

– Joel Osteen.

Day 59

Pains of the Past

Psalms 34:18, "The Lord is close to the brokenhearted and saves those who are crushed in spirit."

Today, I just want you to know that sometimes pains from the past come up in all of our minds. There are triggers in life that make us remember pains of our past and it happens to everyone. In the past few weeks God has spoken to me about pains I've had in my past. God doesn't bring up the hurts to me, but sometimes God will put individuals in my life who would benefit from hearing how I have overcome those pains.

A sweet friend of mine was sharing some hurt that she's had, sexual hurts. She told me how some days she just can't go on and told me that I just wouldn't understand. As much as I wanted to hold back my pain and not bring it up in my memory again, I knew that my pain could help her life, help her to keep living and pursuing God.

I was like her, as are too many women with sexual hurts in their past. I was sexually abused when I was in my late teens after experiencing a sports injury. I was advised to seek out a sport muscle therapist and the therapist took advantage of me in my young, naive age. I was completely devastated. A few weeks after that happened, I received a phone call from the police telling me the tanning salon I visited was under investigation because the owner had planted cameras. Unfortunately images had been streamed online. Those moments I wish I could erase, but I can't. Staying upset won't change the past either, so I needed to find my hope and identity in Christ. He was truly my hope in my time of need (Isaiah 40:31).

A practice that has helped me is to get quiet before the Lord and name the people that abused me out loud. I say their name and then I say, "I forgive you." When we choose to forgive, God hears us. He enriches us with exactly what we need for that day with a perfect measure of grace, energy, and motivation. For all the coffee drinkers out there, myself included, coffee is like forgiveness. It can be complicated to make, but when you get it just right it will make your toes will curl and bring warmth to your heart. I'm sure you're laughing at that statement right now and that's good. The joy of the Lord is our strength, so drink your cup of forgiveness today and put a smile on your face. Choose forgiveness and choose to have fun with your husband and your children (fur babies included too)!

"The moment you asked for forgiveness, God forgave you. Now do your part and leave the guilt behind."

–Joel Osteen

Day 60

Trust in Transition

Proverbs 3:5, "Trust in the Lord with all your heart and do not lean on your own
understanding."

As yet another deployment was approaching, the Marines had to start training for a

new mission. This deployment would be with a MEU. Training for a MEU

deployment means lots of "work-ups". I think I can safely say that all of us wives

can agree that we wish the work-up time counted toward the total time our husband

was deployed away from us. In case you are not familiar with them, work-ups

happen for a number of months right before deployment. It's during these mini-

deployments where he leaves for a few weeks out of each month to train and

practice situations the unit might encounter while on the actual deployment. It's so

hard to see him leave for those training weeks knowing that he is going to be gone

again the next month, and the next month, and then again the next month after that

for a full deployment of at least 6 months after that last work-up.

When this is going on in our lives, it's easy to allow ourselves to become numb to it and not put anything into the relationship anymore. It may be easy to allow that to happen, but we can't do that. We need to choose to make every day count.

Very recently the Marine Corps lost 12 men in a helicopter collision. This time we didn't personally know any of them, although we had been stationed on the same base they were from just prior to the accident. When I heard about it, my heart just broke for those families that had to go through that. With that broken heart I let the realization really sink in, each day really does matter.

Trust God today. Trust him that he will give you the grace to be the kind of wife that your husband is excited to come home to every night. Trust He's watching over your children when they're at school. If you homeschool, trust God will give you the wisdom to teach those children the way He would want you to teach them. If you're a working woman, trust God will give you favor with your bosses and your clientele.

Today, I trust God will speak to you in this devotion. No matter if the world around you is shifting, you are preparing for a move, or maybe your husband is getting ready for deployment and you're going through the same thing I'm going through; trust that God is with you. His love and His grace are unfailing. You're an awesome woman of God. Have a wonderful day today and know God is with you.

He is standing right by your side no matter what kind of transition you are going through. You got this!

"Faith is trusting God even when you don't understand His plan."

-Unknown Author

Day 61

What Do You Think?

Psalms 37:5, "Commit your way to the Lord; trust in him and he will do this."

For my husband's second deployment to Iraq I chose to go to Michigan to stay with my family. I was fixated on finally having close family support since our son was about to turn one years old. Looking back now, I'm so thankful I did. Our son was able to experience having grandparents close since both my parents and my husband's parents lived in the same area in Michigan. There was a lot of work involved in the move, mostly on my part. Once our time in Michigan was over, I had to find an apartment in California, where we were stationed. I wanted to have our belongings from storage moved into the apartment by the time my husband returned. Everything worked out very smoothly, but it definitely took a lot of planning and preparation on my behalf prior to the move.

Sometimes the goals in our life that look so rewarding will also be hard and challenging to achieve.

Remember the story of Naaman from the Bible? He was a commander in the military and said to be a very respected man. Naaman seemed to have it all going for him except for one major problem, he had leprosy. The prophet Elisha was in a nearby town and heard about this man. Elisha had a servant send a letter to tell Naaman to come visit him. Naaman came to the prophet and long story short (my children love this part), did you know what the prophet told Naaman to do? He told Naaman to go to the Jordan River and dip himself seven times for his skin to be cleansed. When Naaman heard what he needed to do he was furious. He didn't want to do it. You see, the Jordan River was known to be beyond filthy during that time. Naaman eventually chose to wash seven times in the river and through his obedience he was made whole (2kings 5:1-19).

Sometimes the things that God wants us to do look really challenging or don't make sense to us. Even though in the end we may want to believe it will pay off, it can still be hard to get our minds wrapped around the hard work it will take to get to the reward. Just remember you're not doing it alone. If God planned it, He will definitely bring it to pass.

Today, challenge yourself. My mom says, "Step out to find out". You will never see the amazing plans God has for you without taking the first step.

"God's plans for my future are far greater than my fears." –Helen Fagan

Day 62

Bullies Named Bill

Philippians 4:13, "I can do all this through him who gives me strength."

Budgeting between you and your spouse can be tough. Who am I kidding, right? It can sometimes be downright stressful. I sat down with my husband one day, we made a budget and he helped me understand the plan. Ladies, I like to shop for my family, but we hit a spot in our life that I needed to hold back. Samuel and I at this point had been married for 11 years. I know what you're thinking, why did it take you guys that long to make a budget? Well, life changed so much that we found ourselves actually needing a good budget. Samuel received a new job placement in the military and even though he was higher in rank in this new placement, we would receive less overall per paycheck. His new job wasn't the only thing to bring the change. We were living in a new state with less BAH. Life happens and things change. We have to learn to change our budgets, and with that, change the way we shop.

Today, I'm not here to preach to you about credit cards or loans. I'm just here to say, take it to God. He wants us to be wise with what He has provided us.

As hard as it is to hold back from going into Hobby Lobby, I had to. Why? Come on, if you know Hobby Lobby you know they always have a 40% off coupon. Secondly, you can always find something you "need" in there. I wanted to go into Hobby Lobby so badly just to shop, but I knew I wouldn't be able to stand the temptation. My (military) big Sis that I met in Hawaii told me that every time she went into Target, she would easily drop three hundred dollars. Women, let's be real for a moment. We know the stores that "get us". Maybe yours is Bass Pro Shop or Barnes and Noble. Whatever your place is, we have to use discretion and wisdom when entering those places. If we don't have the money, we cannot "browse the aisles", it's just not fair to do that to ourselves. Let's be wise women when it comes to the way we spend.

If I can do this, I know you can too. We can both do this, I'm in it with you. No one likes to be bullied, and bills can be the biggest bully in a marriage. Let's ask God to help us today to think before we swipe.

"It's never too late to turn things around. You are the only obstacle."

–Dave Ramsey

Day 63

Wipe Those Paws!

Psalms 51:10, "Create in me a pure heart, O God, and renew a steadfast spirit within me."

How you act today will prepare you for tomorrow's battles. When our husband goes on a deployment, he practices the skills he will need to use during the deployment many times over before he actually leaves. Our husband plans exactly what he's going to take, what weapons he will have, what his source of food will be, and he may need to go over the maps of where he will be or need. There is so much planning that goes into a deployment. We as military wives need to prepare ourselves spiritually. If we are filling up on negative TV and music, well that just isn't going to keep our spirit uplifted. If we are feeding off of that stuff all the time, how can we expect to get through a deployment not depressed? We absolutely can't. When we pour in our lives uplifting and positive teaching and music, we will glow with the knowing that our husband will be safe and we will remain calm. We will have greater peace that God is faithful to His promises. No matter what we see on the news, we will stay calm because we aren't filled up on "average" thinking, we are filled up on God's promises.

We have two dogs, a golden retriever mix and a pekapoo. My family really enjoys having dogs, except maybe when the weather is bad and our pups get filthy when they need to go outside. If we don't use a towel to wipe their paws when they come in, their paw prints will be all over the floor. Just like the towel I keep handy to wipe their paws off, if we have Scriptures and ministry teaching in us and praise on our minds readily available, we are prepared to prevent more of a mess in our lives. We will be ready to identify trouble and give it immediate attention before it runs free through our household. If there is no towel available, we don't let the dogs in until we get one ready. If you know your spirit is in a vulnerable state, why would you let more garbage in through your ears or eyes? The Holy Spirit is our help as he helps convict us of trouble. You won't have to think, "Oh, should I watch this?" or "Should I listen to this?" No, we're prepared with the answer based off the condition of our spirit.

We need to be mindful what we allow to come into our lives. The things we put in our ears and in through our eyes. Just like with our dogs, if we are preventative with wiping their feet in advance, our house will stay clean.

In the same way, our Christian walk will be much cleaner if we are conscious to the things we allow to come in our eyes, ears and out of our mouths.

"You attract what you put out. Be mindful."

–Alexandre Elle

Day 64

On Hold

Isaiah 40:31, "but those who hope in the Lord will renew their strength. They will soar on wings like eagles; they will run and not grow weary, they will walk and not be faint."

My husband and I really wanted to buy a home in California when the market was low in 2009. In April of that year, we started viewing homes and putting in offers. We put in 81 offers, all on different homes (not recommended financial advice). June rolled around, no acceptance yet. July and then August past, nothing was happening. No decisions were being made on the Bank's side of things for the short sale homes. They seemed to be holding out for the market to turn or cash buyers were overbidding us at every turn. The market was so intense during this time with so many short sales and foreclosures in the area. Finally, in September we found out an offer had been accepted on a home. The home we were accepted for was a home we had only seen online pictures of. We had never entered this home in "real life" before we made the offer. The home we bought needed a lot of love and work. The neighbors we were blessed with turned out to be so awesome and we couldn't have been happier with the school district. To top it off, it was located only 5 minutes from the church we were already attending. Turns out God knows us best. He knows the little and the big things that will make us say, "God, how did you know I would want that? It's perfect for me." Being on hold can be so boring, but it's better to be a little bored then extremely unhappy with something you "thought" you wanted.

We need to hold out for the next word from God. Sometimes the thing we're desiring to come true is so close to being fulfilled, but we give up thinking that it's never going to happen too soon. We may even talk ourselves out of it by saying things like, "I guess it wasn't God" or "I guess it's not meant for me." Calm down, you are so close it's not even funny. Remain patient and stay in a praise mindset.

God is never too busy to answer your request, but I am telling you there's a good reason He's having you on hold. It may be because the job just isn't ready for you yet, the perfect one for you and your family. Maybe you're not quite financially prepared for the new house. Whatever is going on, God knows best. God doesn't withhold good from His children (Psalms 84:11). Hold on to the promise

He gave you and be thankful. Praise him every day like that promise has come to pass.

I promise you God will bring them to pass at just the right time in your life. God is never too early or too late, His timing is perfect (Habakkuk 2:3).

"Hold the vision, Trust the process."

–Unknown Author

Day 65

Natural Instinct

2 Corinthian's 8:3, "For I testify that they gave as much as they were able and even be on their ability. Entirely on their own."

To give or not to give? When you're challenged to help others, do you see it as opportunity or a challenge? Or is it just like breathing, a natural instinct?

When we were stationed in California, we attended a wonderful church in Temecula. We had only been going for a month when a couple came up to us and said they would really like to give us one of their cars. Yes, a car! My husband's primary transportation was a motorcycle, come rain or shine. We had wanted him to get a car because he was having too many close calls to and from work. We hadn't talked to anyone about this, it was just something we were hoping for. This couple completely surprised us that morning at church. They said the reason they wanted to give us the car was because over the past few years they have lost a handful of friends due to motorcycle accidents and they knew my husband was depending on his motorcycle for transportation. They wanted him to be safe, especially with the birth of our third baby. Words can't even express how thankful we were for the car, it was a great little car that got us through that period. The couple had a natural instinct to quickly give us one of their cars. They didn't know very much about us. We had only been attending for a short time, but as soon as they found out my husband only had a motorcycle for transportation they wanted to do something about it and they did. They blessed us so much.

For some reading this, you just don't know how to be quick to give because you didn't have any examples of what being a giver looks like. That's okay. God can put that "knowing" in us if we ask Him to show us how to be generous. When we ask God to help us be a blessing to others, He will. At first He will usually suggest something small, like putting your cart away to help the cart guy or girl at the store. Then He will see how quickly you are to respond to that suggestion. From there the suggestions will increase; to buy the lady's coffee behind you and leave a quick note, to make a meal for a needy family. Just as our faith grows each time we choose to use it, so will our natural instinct to be quick to give. Giving feels so good, knowing you are helping someone with their day just makes you live lighter.

"There is no instinct like that of the heart."

-Lord Byron

Day 66

Red Hot

Proverbs 29:22, "An angry man stirs up dissension, and a hot tempered one commits many sins."

When Michael was in the first grade, his teacher had such creative ideas. My favorite idea she had was to make a place in her classroom that was called the "peace place". This place was for students to take a person who offending them and ask them to express why they're offended by the other student face to face. They were then expected to work through it together, peacefully. I just love that. Can you imagine if as married couples we had a peace place when we are having an argument? Wow, that would be amazing. As Christian women of God we can find our peace place. We can go to God to express our anger and hurt or we could even share with him how we regret hurting someone. God will then put within us the right words at the right time and place to make this peace with our husband or others.

We are called to be righteous in God. Anger leads us to sin. When we are filled with anger, we cannot be led to righteousness. Believe me, I'm not saying you can never get angry. What I am saying is we cannot choose to operate in this world anger. As Christians we are supposed to stand out in a good way. If we're acting like other non-Christians by throwing dishes, slamming doors and screaming at our children, or even concealing our anger and letting it influence our attitude, that is not leading us to righteousness.

Yes, I said even concealed anger. When you keep your anger inside, there is no outlet. If you're "that good" about keeping it in and throwing it out the back door, that's awesome. Your ability to forgive is above average. But if you're like most people, myself included, and you choose to conceal it then you have to ask yourself, are you choosing to walk away and think badly towards the other person? If so, that's not the righteous route.

Here is how to get angry righteously; be self-controlled, go to God quickly. Lastly, sometimes this one is the hardest, forgive overlook the offense (Galatians 5:22-23a).

When God calls you to do something, He equips you with the right tools to do those things. With that said, if He calls you to live righteously, He will give you the grace, mercy and the self-control that you need.

Proverbs 14:29, "People with understanding control their anger; a hot temper shows great foolishness."

Day 67

No Filter

Proverbs 18:20, "From the fruit of our mouth a man's stomach is filled; with the harvest from his lips he is satisfied."

Wow, can you imagine if everything we said came true? Think about that for a minute, what did you say when you woke up this morning? Was it something like, "I can't move", or "I'm tired to death!"? I know I am guilty of saying those at one time or another. If everything we said happened, I wouldn't be able to get up and I would literally be as tired as I just confessed. Today I want to remind you that our words matter.

Proverbs 12:18, "Reckless words pierce like a sword, but the tongue of the wise brings healing."

Do you see those pictures on Instagram that have #Nofilter? The same thing can be true about our mouth. Sometimes we are so careless with how we talk that we should put a label right on our forehead saying "#Nofilter".

What is in you? Are you filling up on talk show radio stations or the latest drama about housewives so much that the words those women have spoken over their husband, children, or their own bodies is getting in you? Words of no value get dropped into our mind and into our heart every day when we are allowing the wrong things into our ears.

When we make a habit of listening to certain things, we are going to say things that don't line up with the word of God. We are allowing our days to be filled with uncensored material. We are not truly looking into what we are watching or listening to. Are you taking a step back, looking at the TV and honestly asking yourself, "How is this benefiting my marriage, my children, my family or myself?"

Even when we are filtering what is coming in, we must also allow the Holy Spirit to filter our words and actions coming out. By doing this we are becoming more and more like Jesus. When people look at us, they shouldn't see us. They should see Jesus.

If your words are always encouraging, they're going to uplift someone needing the encouragement that day. If your words are what Proverbs describes as words that "…pierce like a sword," that's not a fun way to love someone. Allow God's word to truly change your words today. Remember the tongue of a fool only cares about their own way (Proverbs 18:7). How are your words? Let's speak the truth and speak in love so that others around us will feel better about their issue through Christ in us.

"Words are free, it's how you use them that may cost you."

—Unknown Author

Day 68

Not Right Now

Ephesians 3:20," Now to him who is able to do immeasurably more than we can ask or imagine according to his power that is at work within us,"

How many of us moms have had to say to our kiddos "Not right now"? I know I do all the time. As a mom, I have legitimate reasons why I can't do what they want me to do in every moment, but from their point of view, they need it right now and we just don't understand them.

Does that sound like you when you're asking God for something in prayer? Do you feel like a child where God is your parent saying "Not yet" because your situation is not changing? I know when I tell my children "Not right now", I know that I'm not saying no, or I would just say no. The same is true with God. We need to stop taking His "Not yet" as a "No". There are reasons why God is having us wait for something.

As an example: My husband wanted this certain career package approved by the military. In his opinion the package would change his military course for the better.

We both came together and prayed for favor and went on a Daniel's fast, asking God to open the door. The results from the board were released and we found out that he wasn't accepted. The week after that, we received orders to move to Kaneohe Bay, Hawaii. We didn't complain or get upset, we stayed focus and did what we had to do to PCS. We knew that God put the package on my husband's heart, and he resubmitted the package two years later and was accepted!

Sometimes we get so frustrated with God. "Why are you doing this, God?" God knows there is a greater good. He knows exactly what you need and when you need it. Just like us moms when we tell our children "Not right now", He has a reason why we're not able to do it right then. We are not always going to explain it to them, we simply need them to trust us. We plan on doing it, we are just prioritizing it. That's just like God, He knows why you can't have what you're asking for right now. It probably doesn't even have anything to do with you, but He is lining up the right people, place, and opportunities just for YOU!

"Just because it's not happening now, doesn't mean it never will."

–Unknown Author

Day 69

Own it!

Psalms 37:23, "The steps of a good man are ordered by the Lord: and he delights in his ways."

God has a calling on your life. Every Christian has a ministry. People hear the word ministry, and we immediately think of pastors and worship leaders. But ministry is really about making disciples. A disciple is someone that follows Jesus wholeheartedly and continues to make more disciples.

If you're saying, "I'm just a mom. I stay home, go to mommy and me classes. How is that a ministry?" Our greatest mission in life can be to show our children Jesus. It's one thing to take our children to church, but it's another thing to live day in and day out as a follower of Jesus.

While we were stationed in North Carolina, we chose to live about 20 miles off base. At times I didn't think it was a good idea because we were in the country. Where we lived we didn't have many neighbors. It was different for us than anywhere else we've been station. One day my 10 year old son approached me and asked, "Why did God bring us here?" I told him that all I know is God wanted us to be here even if it was only to share the love of Jesus with just one person.

Whatever stage you're at in your life right now, whether you are a young mom or you have no children, if your husband is deployed or if he's doing local training events every weekend, don't forget you are there for a reason. The only way to find out the true reason is to dive into God's word. We have to be intentional about our next step. We need to find a local church to be poured into. We need to listen to ministry online or whatever method of hearing the Word that we can make work. We need to fill our heart and our mind with praise, and then we need to pour it all out.

Someone in your community needs you. They need your encouragement and to be able to see what a woman that has a relationship with Jesus truly lives like. Yes, we make mistakes just like everyone else, but then we get back up, dust ourselves off and keep moving forward. God has called you to be exactly where you are, shine your light girl.

Let me pray with you:

Dear God, I pray for my friend, that you would put the right people in her life to minister to her and help her to see the people in her life that she needs to minister too. We are trusting in you, thank you for ordering our steps even before we were born, we love you Lord.

In Jesus' name, Amen.

Day 70

Stronger than Ever

Haggai 2:9, "The glory of this present house will be greater than the glory of the former house,' says the Lord Almighty. And in this place I will grant peace."

Births, birthdays, all the "firsts", holidays and anniversaries are all special times of the year and I know all too well the sadness that we can have at those times when we are without our husband. I am blessed that my husband was home for all three of our babies' births, but I can relate for all the other missed events a few times over. My husband has missed so much of the major events in our children's lives. My heart hurts for him as I know he desperately wanted to be there for all those times. I remember one time when he missed the boys' third year of flag football, I kind of felt pressured by my husband to make sure I was "videoing every play during the games". Sounds funny to say, but I'm sure you can probably relate.

When we were stationed in Hawaii, I applied for our two boys to go to a small local school. You had to enter into a lottery to have your children placed on a waiting list. I wasn't notified until three days before the start date of school that our boys were accepted! I was so excited but wasn't able to share the excitement with my husband due to him being away. It's even in those little times that I wish he could celebrate with me. I had to email him to tell him the great news. When he emailed me back he told me that he wished he was home so he could take us out to dinner in order to celebrate. I could tell he was very disappointed by not being able to be home, I reassured him we would take a rain check for when he got back. It is frustrating sometimes not being able to experience everything together, but just remember God truly has you both during those times.

I believe we will have the time made up to us for all the missed moments our spouses are away if we stay rooted in Christ. Yes he is gone so long, but when he gets back, instead of filling the house with disagreements or arguments on who should take the trash out, we can fill our homes with laughter and understanding. We have all gone through a lot during separation and we each have grown in separate ways, but when we are reunited the bond between us will be stronger than ever before.

"Always remember that your present situation is not your final destination, the best is yet to come."

−Zig Ziglar

Day 71

Do You See What God Sees in You?

Isaiah 41:10a, "Don't be afraid, for I am with you."

Let me tell you this much I know to be true, being married to my Marine I know God is with me each day. I am here to tell you that God is with you, too. I know at times it is hard to be a military spouse, bills don't get paid because we just forget with everything else that's going on, we have to be the only parent at the school conference, and we are often the only cheerleader or coach for our children because their daddy is away. Through it all, God sees you full of strength and beautiful from the inside out.

He sees you sitting on the floor with your children folding clothes while they are watching their favorite show. He sees you working hard through multiple jobs. He sees you taking your husband to work because you only have one car. He sees you trying to motivate yourself through the day because you woke up with a bad insulin port. He sees you as you take your children to the doctors. He sees you if you're crying out to Him (right now) because your husband just left on

179

deployment. He sees you if you're halfway through the deployment and it just doesn't feel like you can take it any longer. Friend, He sees you!

I hope you can feel His heartbeat. He longs to be close to you, especially during those times when your husband is away. Right now as you're reading, please know my eyes are dripping with tears because I might not see you as He sees you, but my heart feels for you. I know times can be hard, believe me I've been there, but know that God wants to be near you to comfort you. Ask God to walk with you today. He will give you the strength, grace and mercy that you need.

I wish somehow as you're reading this I could be sitting right next to you to give you a military sister hug, but I have hope that you can feel it. You've got this girl, no matter what is thrown in your lap… you've "got" this.

Let me pray with you:

Dear Lord, I pray that you be with my friend today. Give her the strength that only you can give. Embrace her and give her the comfort she needs when her nights are lonely while her husband is away. Strengthen her, Lord. Give her the grace to do exactly what she needs to do. Thank you for the bond we have to each other through the military, that we can truly call each other sisters, sisters in Christ and sisters in our similar military paths. We love you Lord.

In Jesus' name, Amen.

Day 72

It Hurts!

Psalms 143:1, "Lord, hear my prayer, listen to my cry for mercy; in your faithfulness and righteousness come to my relief."

Sometimes when I put in a good workout, I don't always feel anything that same day. Then the next morning I wake up like, "Wow this hurts! Why did I do that to myself?" I know that usually any hurt is a good hurt because it means I worked out that part of my body where I'm trying to build muscle.

Sometimes the battles we face in life hurt. Sometimes it feels like we've been punched in the gut, like when your husband is deployed to a dangerous location and you know there will be no communication with him for a while. As hard as it is knowing that your best friend is going to be away from you, believe me when I say it will make you stronger. If someone would have said that to me in our first deployment, I would have wanted to smack them, let's just be real. To my surprise, however, that first deployment strengthened me and also strengthened my marriage. My husband wasn't able to call me for more than a few days into our first deployment since being married. It was tough, especially seeing countless images of what was going on through the various news networks at that time. My faith grew and I became closer to God than I had ever been in my life as I was desperately reliant on God.

With each deployment, you will experience more of God's goodness; He has you. He is protecting both you and your husband. Choose to focus on God's goodness instead of the hurt, you will have more peace than you have ever imagined. How do you experience peace during a deployment? One way is by choosing to prepare yourself in the Lord before the deployment or work-ups even start. I encourage you to soak yourself up in the Word of God prior to your husband even leaving. Make time for God by spending time in His Word. I'm not saying you won't feel any pain with your husband's absence, however, when you start the deployment you will have more confidence in God that you know this deployment will not bring harm. You won't have a panic attack and get all crazy in your tissues. No, you will be more prepared emotionally. God's grace will cover you and you will truly see Him at work in your life. He will comfort you and give you the peace you need to establish a great new routine while your husband is away (Trust me, if He did it for me He wants to do that for you too).

One thing I have found helpful is writing down my thoughts during deployments, even if it's just a quick sentence like, "Today stinks". It helps me look back over how I responded during the last deployment and it helps me find the motivation to get through the next one. It's important to remember what God has brought us through because it reminds us of God's faithfulness. If He did it before, He will definitely bring us through the next one (Psalms 143).

"Life is hard, but God is good."

–Unknown Author

Day 73

Fasting

Philippians 4:13, "I can do all things through Christ who gives me strength."

You've probably heard of people fasting. If you haven't, fasting is when you give up something that you enjoy for a period of time (days, weeks, years, forever) and you instead devote that time to prayer and scriptures. You sacrifice something in your life to your own hurt to commit that time to speaking and listening to God as well showing God you are committed to whatever it will take to get the breakthrough you need for a specific situation. I know some say fasting is "too extreme" or that it's a waste of time because we can't force God to answer us. Well, I believe it's a very normal thing for Christians to do and I realize we can't force God to answer to us like that. However, I do know when you're fasting it shows God that we are really putting Him first over our own fleshly desires.

People fast different things. Some people fast social media, watching television, or go completely without food. Some people only eat nutritious liquids and some do what has been called the Daniel's Fast. I usually do The Daniel's Fast. The

Daniel's Fast is when you cut out all products with added sugar and you pretty much just eat fruits and vegetables. I remember one time my husband was away at training during a particular fast. I really felt like I was going completely without a lot of things that I love and hold dear during that particular time. I don't say that to lift myself up or to tell you about something I have accomplished but to encourage both you and me to keep fasting as a tool we use to strengthen our relationship with God, no matter what our situation is.

Let me share one experience I have had with fasting. During this fast, I was getting a workout in at home. Before the fast, I had been feeling very defeated. I wasn't finding work as quickly as I had in the past after a recent PCS. Things just were not clicking for me in a lot of areas. I was running on a treadmill when a song came on. It was a song that made me just want to dance. While I was dancing, I began to have this feeling of God's presence rush over me. The feeling just felt so wonderful. In that moment on the treadmill, I felt God's love rush over me, kind of like a cool breeze. I began to dance around my bedroom and into my children's rooms. Then I began to cry happy tears. I began to speak out loud thanking God for everything that he's already done for me, the children that I have, for my awesome beyond gorgeous husband that I have, and for my faith. In that moment I felt His joy come back into my life, something that I think I had been missing for a few months. I won't ever forget that moment. His joy is something so sweet, it's like a funny movie that just keeps you smiling.

Today, search your heart. Ask God if fasting is something that you should do. Even if it's just fasting television or social media and replacing that time to read God's word. Fasting is such a wonderful experience.

"Fasting coupled with mighty prayer is powerful."

-Joseph B. Wirthlin

Day 74

Why?

Psalms 119:114, "You are my refuge and my shield; I have put my hope in your word."

For you mom's out there, yes even you fur-moms, I'm sure you've said this word at least 10 times just this week: "Why did you do that!?" It just rolls off our tongue as if we are actually looking for a real answer. I'll never forget a time when our second born son was 2 years old. He was playing on the floor one moment than suddenly vanished. I frantically began to look around the inside of our house. When I found him he was under the vanity of the bathroom sink trying to eat Desitin, you know, the rash cream. In what couldn't have been more than 2 minutes, he had smeared it all over his legs, arms and mouth. I quickly cleaned him up while also calling a poison control center. Thankfully he was fine and they just instructed me to have him drink some milk. Another time after he had turned 4 years old, I was keeping an eye on him while he was having fun trying to blow up a balloon. I watched helplessly in slow motion as I saw him put the balloon up to his lips and quickly inhale right before my eyes. The balloon disappeared into his mouth and I instantly freaked out! I screamed, "Why did you suck it in?!" His laughing response, "I don't know". Having added the number to my speed dial years earlier, I quickly made another call to the poison control center. This time they instructed me to keep a close eye on his breathing, have him drink some milk and look for the balloon in his stool until it passed.

Why do I share those interesting stories with you? Am I advertising milk? No, when we are going through our day and different issues come up we tend to focus more on asking God, "Why is this happening to me?" instead of asking God, "How can I grow in this area in my life?" We all get stumped sometimes in life when we constantly feel pressure from the same issues; college debt seems out of control, your husband's job is driving you a little crazy. There are many things that can cause us to question God's faithfulness, that's when we need to bring into remembrance all the times he has been faithful.

Today, instead of asking God, "Why?" Turn that into, "God, how can I allow this to increase my faith and my trust in you?" God will see your sincere heart and he'll give you the wisdom you need for that area. Remember, God is on your side. He will give you the wisdom you need for the frustrating situation in front of you. God will not allow anything to break you, He is a good Father and will walk you through the toughest of times.

"Sometimes when you wonder why you can't hear God's voice during your trails.

Remember the teacher is always quiet during the test."

-Unknown Author

Day 75

Strike Zone

Jonah 1:3, "But Jonah got up and went in the opposite direction to get away from the Lord."

Recently I started participating in the all spouse kickball team at my husband's squadron. I am definitely not as athletic as I once was in my childhood days when I played on different soccer teams, but I remember how to kick a ball just fine. At the first game of the season the more experienced players felt they needed to remind me, the rookie, to kick the ball when the ball crossed into the batter's box with the home plate. Before the game started they made sure to repeatedly tell me I must kick the ball while in the strike zone or it would be considered a strike and that strikes are not a good thing. While watching my other awesome teammates take their turn, I related that thought to spiritual context, how some of us feel we've missed our opportunity, we've missed our window for what God wanted us to do in our life.

When I was in my late teens I made some not great choices with the people I was hanging out with. They were some very sweet girls, but they were not following after the things of God. I was noticing myself slipping up in how I would talk and act. When I felt God was putting something on my heart to do, I would blow Him off like, "Not now God. I'm too busy having fun." Sometimes when we are in sin we don't realize how much it is setting us back until our sin catches up to us. God is such a loving Father, even when I messed up with how I was acting, He never left me. When I realized that how I was living wasn't Godly, far from it in fact, I knew I needed to repent. Even though I repented of my sins, I felt I missed open doors God presented to me while I was not fully committed to Him. He had thrown a beautiful pitch, but I got a strike.

God is bigger than anything. He is so big that even though I had messed up the original timing, He later gave me the same beautiful plan for my life, just with a different beginning date. God was waiting for me to be ready for the next pitch He had, the pitch He always intended for me to kick out of the park.

Friend, God is there for you in the same way, saying to you "Are you ready to take the next pitch?"

"How beautiful it is that God still pursues us when we are running from Him."

–Unknown Author

Day 76

Clothes Off

1 Peter 4:8, "Above all, love each other deeply, because love covers over a

multitude of sins."

My husband and I attended a marriage conference in Irvine, California back in 2012. We had such a great time and learned a few things about each other. One of the speakers, Jimmy Evans, said something that has stuck with us over the years. He said, "Whenever you're in an argument with your spouse, don't argue with your clothes on." My husband and I got such a kick out of that. It's true. How can you still be mad when you're both naked?

Disagreements in a marriage happen. Whether it's over finances, the children's daycare schedule or the in- laws, they just happen. Why? Well, because you both are not an exact clone of each other. You are each different and you're married to help each other see different sides and come together in agreement during conflict.

In our marriage, Samuel is a genius when it comes to finances. I, on the other hand, will admit I'm not that hot! He just has a way with making great spreadsheets and documenting a fancy budget. I have always loved to be a giver, even if it means I have to do without something for a while. Samuel has really showed me that yes we can give, but we need to be good stewards of what God has given us too. We must ensure that we give and commit to things that only God wants us to be a part of, not things we are hyped up for. If it's of God, He will provide a way for it to be. We need to be good stewards of what God has given us for when there are situations we haven't planned for when He calls us to give. Like the moment in church the Pastor asked us to support a child through Compassion International Ministries, I turned to my husband and said, "Can we!?" He said, "I don't know why we wouldn't." I knew he had our budget so greatly planned that I needed to ask him first, marriage is about team work and working together. I didn't want to make a promise I couldn't keep or fail in a commitment which could hurt my family and this little boy overseas. When my husband was last deployed he really put his trust in me to keep the finances running smoothly, especially when we wouldn't be able to communicate for a long stretch. Before a deployment happens, my husband goes over with me where the money needs to be focused and what bills we really need to reduce or get rid of. Even though we are all pretty good about getting the Power of Attorney paperwork completed before our husband deploys, it's a great idea to sit and agree on some kind of budget together. Believe me, I know how hard planning a budget is. Sometimes it even makes my stomach hurt, but being prepared and in agreement really makes that area work for both of us much smoother.

Remember, you're meant to sharpen each other (Proverbs 7:27). You're his helpmate and he is yours! When an argument comes up, even in finances, remember that life is too short, friend, don't let yourself stay mad. Argue with your clothes off!

"Marriage is a partnership, and couples can't win with money unless they're doing the budget as a team."

–Dave Ramsey

Day 77

But I Just Miss Him

Isaiah 41:10a, "So do not fear, for I am with you..."

One night when my husband was away Adella was having a really hard night. She kept crying and saying, "I miss my daddy." My heart ached for her because I knew exactly how she felt. Even though our husbands are away we have the assurance that God is always with us. I know that may sound "religious" but it's so true. He is always right there with you.

This may be your first deployment you have had to go through apart from each other and you just don't see how you can go on with your life by yourself. Friend, I was there too, first deployments are such an adjustment. Will it get any easier? I wish I could answer that for you. For me, over the years it hasn't gotten any easier. However, I can say God gives me the wisdom I need to find a good routine; from activities to do with my children to small projects to keep my brain busy.

Routine is key during a deployment. If you don't work or have little ones, you need to find something productive to occupy your time. No matter what, stay plugged into your local church. You can't say, "Well, I'm not going to church without him. That will be too hard." No, you need the church. You need to go to God with other believers and press into all God has for you.

I don't even want to imagine what would happen if we allowed ourselves to fill the void within us by filling it with worldly ways; partying, over spending or eating. Our choices during a deployment can have positive effects on our marriage or it can have a really nasty effect on our marriage. We choose what our husband comes home to. We are either going to be the wife that is kissing him all over and more on fire for Christ (and probably even holding a fun welcome home sign), or sadly we are going to be the wife that is covered in sadness because she is ashamed of herself for making poor choices during his absence.

Take a deep breath. You, my friend are graced for this. You are capable of so much more. Allow yourself to be so consumed by God's grace that you find yourself knowing you are doing exactly what you were made for. You were made for this.

"I started missing you the moment you said goodbye."

–Unknown Author

Day 78

Deployment Blues

Romans 8:28b, "And we know that in all things God works for the good of those who love Him, ..."

It seems like every deployment I hear the spouses around me talking about the "deployment curse." When something breaks or doesn't go the way we plan, it's easy to blame it on the deployment curse. On our fifth deployment, the day my husband left, for whatever reason I was unable to log in to our online bank account access. A message kept popping up saying that I wasn't an account holder. I found myself saying, "Here we go again. The deployment curse has struck again." I couldn't believe I had said it out loud. Here I am knowing God is fully with me and has only promised me good, not bad, and I was saying that I was being hit by a curse. Friend, things happen. Things break. Things happen when our husband is with us too, but because he is with us we don't see it as being as bad because he can help us through or deal with it themselves. When they're away we don't have that extra support and it's easy to fall into the trap of labeling it as a curse.

When my husband, Mr. Fix-it, was on a deployment, here is a list of things that broke within just the first month of him being away.

1. My van's driver side power window stopped working. You know how annoying that can be with how many times we have to go on and off base, showing our I.D. to the gate guards?

2. The van's gas tank lid bent so I could not open it when I was at a gas station out of town.

3. My van's side front tire became so flat during a little road trip that it resulted in me having to replace both front tires before I could continue the drive.

4. The tailgate door supports stopped working, so it would slam shut and not stay open on its own, I had to find a broom to hold it open.

5. After giving up on my van, I switched to my husband's truck, then his gas cap broke off in my hand as I was trying to fill the tank.

6. The house which we were renting had the air conditioning unit stopped working at the beginning of the summer months.

Crazy right? Things happen and I'm sure you can relate. We can choose to go through the troubling times with God's help and take steps to resolve the issues, or we can choose to be defeated.

Let's choose to take the negative things that come up and take them on with God's grace. We can do this, God is with you!

"Don't worry about tomorrow, God is already there."

−Unknown Author

Day 79

Distractions

Proverbs 4:27, "Do not turn to the right or the left; keep your foot from evil."

What is a distraction? Distractions are something that prevents someone from giving full attention to something else. If you're a mom you know what this looks like, you're trying to make an important phone call and your little one isn't understanding what it means when you shake your head at them. It's hard for women, especially moms of little ones, to find time to give full attention to one thing.

Do you remember the story of Mary and Martha? Martha, as many of us wives would be, was busy in the kitchen preparing meals (and I'm sure cleaning up as she went). Mary just sat at Jesus' feet while Martha was frustrated in the kitchen making everything perfect for their guests. Jesus said something like this to Martha, "You're fussing too much and getting yourself worked up over nothing." Has your husband ever said that to you? I know mine has. When we were first married I would get worked up over having anyone over. Everything had to be freshly cleaned. Jesus was telling Martha that Mary was doing exactly what they both should be doing and that was being with Him (Luke 10:38-42).

Life can be full to the max with work events and children's activities. It's our responsibility to determine what things, what events matter. If we are spending so much time on the computer for work and not giving first place in the morning to God with devotion time, we are allowing ourselves to become distracted. I had an older mom with four children tell me, "God has given you grace. Some days you need to give yourself some grace, too." She was so right, as military spouses we have so much going on. When our husband is away, there is so much more pressure added on to what already rests on our shoulders. We truly need to stop ourselves from becoming so caught up in what "has to be done" instead of what is most important, our time with God being the highest priority.

So today ask yourself if you are becoming distracted from something that is taking time away from God. Remember, distractions can even become camouflage, so be on guard. At times it won't even be a bad distraction, it can appear like something as sweet and good looking as volunteering too much or signing up for too many events. Ask God to help you clearly identify if you have unneeded distractions so that you can remove them.

It may be difficult to say no to some things, or someone, but if you keep saying yes to everyone you won't be able to say yes to the things God is really needing you to do.

"You can't do BIG things if you're distracted by SMALL things."

–Unknown Author

Day 80

Mouth Guard

Proverbs 21:35, "He who guards his mouth and tongue keeps himself from trouble."

Do you have that someone in your life that you sometimes wish you had a mute button for because all they seem to do is speak negative? As funny as that sounds, sometimes the person that needs to be muted or restrained is us. Psalms 141:3 says, "Set a guard over my mouth, Lord; keep watch over the door of my lips."

Have you seen the movie, "Alexander and the Terrible, Horrible, No Good, Very Bad Day"? At the start of the movie, Alexander always seemed to have a rough day. To him, it seemed as though his family members always had a perfect day. On the night before his birthday he made a wish that his family would have just one day of disappointment so they would understand his life. Needless to say, his wish came true. Each of his family members, even down to the baby, had a completely awful day. As funny as the movie was, it's a good reminder that the things we say can make our day radiant or ridiculous.

As spouses, we should know how the things people say can affect other people and the environment in our home. Living on base can be a wonderful or awful experience. It really depends on if you are able to surround yourself with positive people as influences in your life and who is living in the home next to you. One day, I caught myself not talking very great about another spouse, it was almost like I had an out of body experience. It just came out and I couldn't believe what I was hearing myself say. In that moment, I quickly changed where the conversation was going. Yes, it's easy to get onboard the gossip train; however, we need to keep a watch on our mouths. Similar to Alexander from the movie, we too can cause someone's day to go bad or we can choose to speak life into the ones around us. What if the spouse we were mentioning walked up at that very moment? Her day would have been shattered. She would have replayed the event over and over before that same evening was over. There are all kinds of possible negative consequences to the words we chose to use.

We know too well what it's like to be talked about or even to be caught up in a conversation with a negative person; it's no fun. Today, let's ask God to help us guard our mouth. Let's be encouragers!

"Your words can be powerful, they can hurt or uplift, so think before you speak, as every word you say counts." – Leon Brown

Day 81

Don't Yell, Come to Me!

Psalms 34:19a, "The righteous cry out, and the Lord hears them; ... "

"Don't yell! Come to me!" is a common saying around our house. My children would always yell "Mom!!" and then try to talk and ask us questions from far away, even when they can't see us. When this first started happening I would get very frustrated with it, but now I don't even yell back an answer. I simply say in a normal voice, "Don't yell. Come to me." At one of those times, I had a thought. I wonder if God ever thinks about that when we yell to him for something. "God, why didn't you heal my mom?! Why didn't you help us pay our rent this month?! God, where were you?!" It's almost like we are yelling at him. I wonder if He says the same words that I say to my children, "Don't yell. Just come to me."

If we went to God by opening up His Word to see what He has already said about a situation or we made time just to spend talking with Him instead of whining at Him, I wonder how much more we would accomplish in our spiritual lives. It sounds so simple to just get a little closer to God. He will not push His way into our lives. He is waiting to be invited, not screamed at. We should be talking to God just like we do our closest friends. When you go to God He is always ready listen.

Matthew 6:33, "But seek first his kingdom and his righteousness, and all these things will be given to you as well."

When we seek God and truly go after the things He wants us to go after, doors will be opened to you like never before. Big breaks will happen for you. Others around you will scratch their heads and ask, "How did that happen for you?" You can say it was all God. When we seek Him and His ways, we find Him. We find the plan He designed for us from before we were born. It's such an exciting time when you know you're exactly where you need to be and you're doing exactly what you were created to do, all because you kept seeking Him.

Go to God today and bring your needs and desires to Him. Simply seek him, speak your mind to Him like you are face to face. When we seek Him, we always find Him because He's always been there just waiting for us to come to Him for direction.

"Don't stop praying. He hears you and He is working it out for your good."

–Unknown Author

Day 82

Snowman Hotdogs

Ephesians 4:7,"However, he has given each one of us a special gift through the generosity of Christ."

One day Michael asked me to make snowman hotdogs. As a mom I'm simply thinking "Snowman hotdogs? How is that possible?" I had no idea what he was talking about at first. Was it something he had a dream about and there was a snowman shaped like a hotdog? He was only three at the time he asked for that. I racked my brain and quickly came up with an idea how I could turn a hotdog into a snowman. I begin creating a way to chop up a hot dog, stack it like a snowman, and decorated it with toothpicks and ketchup. It actually turned out ok, but to my three-year-old it was awesome!

At a Mommy and Me class I attended, there was a mom we'll call Betty. She would get so frustrated by this other mom, Macy who would always come to class with her daughter dressed in the cutest little dress she had handmade for her. Betty would get so annoyed with Macy's creativity that she would be so mean to her with the expressions and comments she made toward her. It was so sad to see this happening out of what looked like apparent jealousy over someone else's creativity ability.

Believe it or not, both of these stories are related. I wanted to share them both with you as examples of being creative and graced in different ways. We are all blessed with different ways in which we are graced. In Macy's case, she just happened to be able to sew anything she could imagine. Betty had gifting's of her own as well. She always looked nice, she bought her son the cutest little boy outfits, and she always brought in a fun snack to share, to name a few.

In sharing these stories, I challenge you to examine your heart. Are you more likely to become frustrated when another wife seems to have her house always clean, or her kiddos always matching. How about if her hair and makeup are always done? Instead of getting so frustrated, think about yourself and what are you good at? When you know what you're good at you can achieve more than when you choose to be frustrated at somebody else's creativity and what they are graced with.

If you're like Macy, don't get discouraged when other women around you get frustrated because you can do something that they can't. God has gifted you with the abilities you have. If you stop doing what God has called you to do just so you can try to please other people, then you will not be fulfilling your purpose that God designed you for!

I know this one can be challenging for us moms to read. When we get excited and celebrate someone else when they accomplish great things, God will bless us in our own gifting's even more.

Examine your heart today, examine yourself and ask God to show you exactly what you are graced to do. God has given each of us an amazing gifting or talent, it's our job to find out what that is and to practice it. Don't put other people down because they seem to have their gifting down pat. Instead, examine yourself and pray. Seek God's face and have Him show you what your gifting is. I am praying over you today that God will give you wisdom beyond your years, that you will know exactly what you are called to do and that you will have the courage to practice it without hesitation.

"The worst enemy to creativity is self-doubt."

–Sylvia Plath

Day 83

Relief

Hebrews 11:1, "Now faith is confidence in what we hope for and assurance about what we do not see."

When my husband was to arrive home from his fourth deployment, our children and I waited patiently for him at the squadron. It was one of those times when minutes felt like hours, when the buses pull up with all the Marines returning from deployment and you know your spouse is sitting in one of those seats. Your heart is filled with relief that all of the phone calls that were made, all the face timing and all the packages sent are at an end because he is finally home! Nothing can compare to that feeling of knowing that he is about to be right in front of you ready to give you guys the biggest hug in the world! Even now the thought makes me smile and tear up all at the same time as I know we are approaching another deployment this year. I would much rather fast forward to that day when the buses pull up!

When we are waiting for a dream to come to pass it's easy to find ourselves complaining about our current circumstances. We start questioning ourselves and maybe even questioning God's Word and timing. Why is this taking so long?! It often feels like we live in such a fast paced world, I mean imagine when our parents were children. I'm sure you've heard some of the same stories I have, like, "Cable TV? With over one hundred channels? Back when I was your age I only had one channel and it was in black in white." Or, "Fast food?! My mom had six children to feed. It would take her all day to prepare dinner!" We have to remember some things we want an immediate response to may be something that needs to be prepared for us. In Ecclesiastes 3:11 we read, "He has made everything beautiful in its time..." It's His timing we need to patiently wait for. It's truly in Him where He sets the timing up so perfectly, but it requires waiting. Relief will come. Hang in there, and while you are waiting dig deeper into His Word.

Psalm 46:5, "She believed she could so she did."

Day 84

Minivan... No Way!

Psalm 16:5, "You, Lord, are all I have, and you give me all I need; my future is in your hands"

When I was a teenager I said I would never own a minivan. Well, when Adella was born we were driving a small SUV. Every time I had to leave the house it was a struggle. Having to buckle all three babies into their seats and still having to load the massive three-seat stroller in the back (let's not forget I had to leave room for the groceries!). It was in those hectic times I began to realize I would have to get the vehicle that I needed and not one that I just wanted. Giving in to owning a minivan completely helped out. I didn't have to figure things out when it came to transportation and errands anymore. A stressful routine was made simple. When we make decisions based on our needs over our wants, it's a good feeling after we know we've made the right decision. We may get some ridicule for not doing (or driving) the cool thing. However, when we know we've made our decision based on all the good reasons we will find it comes easy to throw out any ridicule.

The same is true with our walk with Christ. A lot of people say, "Oh, you just want to have a crutch to lean on when you want something." A relationship with Jesus isn't just something nice we should want to have around, it is something that we all need in our lives. When someone can actually look at me in my eyes and tell me that they don't need Christ, my heart hurts for them because I don't know how they are going to make it on this earth without truly knowing Him. Having God with me is the only reason I have made it through different times of my life (the great and the not so great times).

God is always there for us. It is when we make the decision to say, "Yes God, I need you. I can't do this life without you.", that we can begin to experience the fullness of His power at work in our lives. Even through the messiness of life, God is with us. He is walking us through until we reach the other side. When we push our own understanding aside for His truths, He will make our lives much easier to face because He knows better. We must make Christ our number one source for everything (Proverbs 3:5-6).

When you put Christ first you're saying yes to His ways, yes to His provision and yes to His healing. Today let's clear off our list of wants and make a declaration that says I am starting fresh, and making Him my #1 need.

All other desires will fall into place when we allow ourselves so be dependent on God for everything.

"I am not ashamed to say how desperately I need Jesus in my life."

–Unknown Author

Day 85

Little by Little

Psalms 37:23, "The Lord directs the steps of the godly. He delights in every detail of their lives."

Do you have a dream that you've wanted to see fulfilled for a long time? Examples as big as: getting out of debt, going back to school, getting your GED, or maybe even starting your own business? It's so easy to allow the busyness of life to hold us back from seeing our dreams fulfilled. Believe me, as challenging as it can be between the many different military moves and normal every day responsibilities, we have to devote some time to building ourselves and fulfilling the dream that God has put within us! Life is too short to live in the moment, we have to make time count for us and not against us.

MSN.com made available studies from different research teams which show how an average person spends their time over a 75 year period. I have listed a few of the things that really stuck out to me.

- 26 years sleeping (According to Organization for Economic Co-operation and Development)

- 38 hours per year in traffic (According to Texas A&M annual mobility)

- 4.4 years eating

- 8.5 years on shopping

- 1 year deciding what to wear (According to a survey by clothing company Matalan)

- 10.3 years working (According to an American study)

- 11 years watching TV

- 5 months complaining (According to a poll by Hilary Blinds)

- 7 years lying awake (According to Canadian health experts)

- 4 years talking on the phone while at work (According to Working Lives researchers)

- 115 days laughing

- 3 years washing clothes (According to Newstrategist research)

- 136 days on getting ready (study from body wash firm, Skinbliss).

Wow, and just like that our 75 years of life are over. I know that may sound a little morbid but friend, we truly need to make our time count. It starts with the little things we do every day that can add up to a big accomplishment. I know it's tough to start taking the necessary steps needed to complete a dream but the rewards will completely pay off and that's so exciting!

As you take the little steps toward your dream, God blesses them. As I shared with you earlier in this devotional, I always wanted to be a wife and a mom. When that dream came to pass, God placed another dream on my heart. I wasn't able to see how the dream was going to come to pass until a few years ago, but each day I woke up and did my best to complete the small step He needed me to do for that day.

Remember, in the back of this book there is a page just for you to write your vison. Friend, I urge you…Don't put off the dreams any longer. Take the small steps that you can each day and you will fulfill that big dream that God has placed on your heart. I'm excited for you! This is your time!

"Never let go of your dreams."

–Unknown Author

For the full report of how people spend 75 years of their life, go to the following website: https://www.msn.com/en-gb/lifestyle/life/30-surprising-facts-about-how-we-spend-our-time/ss-BBjeV3f#image=31. Article: "30 surprising facts about how we spend our time." May 4, 2015.

Day 86

You're My Source

Matthew 18:3, "And he said... unless you change and become like little children, you will never enter the kingdom of heaven."

Are you asking the right source for help? Sometimes we get so caught up on how much we make in a paycheck that we take a foot out of our faith walk and dangle it in the world. Friend, the world gets their ideas from media and the latest trends. We, as Christian women of God, need to seek Jesus first. When you were a child, you reached out for your parent or guardian. You're an adult now. It's time to reach out to the only source—Father God. He truly wants the best for you and has unlimited resources to make it happen.

When I was 18 years old, I was in a car accident. It was raining and I was all by myself. The man I hit didn't care about his car and left immediately, but my car was completely totaled. I was a crying mess and called my dad. He said to me, "What were you going to do before your accident?" I told him I was going shopping. My dad told me to park the car and go into the local stores near where I was located and he would be there soon to take care of it. I knew my dad would know exactly what to do, and I relied on my dad to talk to the insurance agency and police. I had no question that my dad could help me. I knew he was the perfect source for my crisis.

I share that story with you because there are times when the military lifestyle can leave you completely in a fog and you want to run into your husband's arms for help, only your husband is hundreds or thousands of miles away. In those times, remember God is always there for you. We need to completely rely on Jesus as our source, running to Him first instead of last. We need to turn to Jesus automatically, our number one source. There will be times when you feel overwhelmed and have to make huge decisions without your spouse to help you. God will not only guide you to make the right decision, but also provide you with the peace to follow through with it.

One time when my husband was deployed to the Middle East with a MEU, part of the plastic casing covering the bottom area of the engine of my van fell apart while I was driving around and I couldn't call him for help. We didn't have the extra money to go get it fixed, so I had to think of something. I know God gave me the grace, wisdom, and zip ties to perform a satisfactory fix for the casing.

This was just a simple situation, but God will give you the know how to do so much more than you ever thought you would be capable of doing. Turn to Him as your source in every situation.

"God is your source. Everything else is just a resource."

–Tony Evans

Day 87

First

Proverbs 3:9-10, "Trust God from the bottom of your heart; don't try to figure out everything on your own. Listen for God's voice in everything you do, everywhere you go; he's the one who will keep you on track. Don't assume that you know it all. Run to God! Run from evil! Your body will glow with health, your very bones will vibrate with life!" – The Message Bible

We can sing the song "I Surrender All" until we are blue in the face, but when push comes to shove are we really surrendering all of ourselves? God has asked us to put him first in every area in our lives. Not so we would be glorified, but so God would be glorified. Tithing is an easy measure of your commitment to put God first (Malachi 3:10).

Since my husband and I have been married, we have committed to be tithers. My husband has always been so great about giving God our first earnings. When tight financial situations come, he has always said, "Tithing isn't an option." There have been so many times where things have changed to our favor for no "real" reason, it's just God's favor. We both contribute these unimaginable blessings to our tithing.

After having children, a common physical reaction is for your teeth to become brittle and more sensitive to cavities. I had great dental hygiene, but after having our last child my teeth needed so much work. The dentist told me I needed several teeth filled and that the total to get white fillings would be nearly $2000 or getting the silver fillings instead would only be $900. I told them that I needed to go with the silver because I'm a mom of three with a tight budget and their needs are priority right now. He shook his head and tried to convince me the white would look so much better. I told him I completely understand, but at this point I just couldn't have the white done. He went away for a moment and came back to start the work. He tapped my shoulder and said, I've never done this before, but I just can't put silver in your mouth, I am giving you the white for the same price. Tears rolled down my face as I tried to say thank you with a numb mouth.

In that moment, the dentist didn't really know why he was giving me that awesome deal, but God did. God can even put things on the hearts of un-saved to bring you favor.

When we obey and give God what He has requested of us, He sees your heart. He sees that you are putting Him first.

"Tithing is entry-level obedience."

- Jason Brinker

Day 88

Leaks

Psalm 139:23-24, "Investigate my life, O God, find out everything about me;
Cross-examine and test me, get a clear picture of what I'm about; See for yourself
whether I've done anything wrong...then guide me on the road to eternal life." –
The Message Bible

We had a major leak in our house that we owned and rented out from our time in California. Of course Sam was deployed, again. I had to have a plumber go and do a leak detection test. The leak detection test helps determine the origin of the leak. A leak can be caused by many things, this day in particular, the leak was due to the tenant putting a lot of raw meat down the kitchen sink. So much meat that it caused the pipe to clog, pressure to build up and the pipe to rupture.

Leaks can happen in our spiritual walk too, we need to perform a leak detection test on our spiritual mind to see if there are areas that are being overloaded by the world's demands.

Your leak detection test may show that you're volunteering too much at your child's school and God wants you to put more time into working on the book that he needs you to write. It might be that He wants you to put your time into volunteering at your church. Your test could show that you're putting too much pressure on your husband to be more romantic and that you need to just love on him right now for where he is at emotionally. Maybe you're being too hard or critical on your child and need to ease up just a little bit.

Let's choose today to not fail where it matters most. Locate the leaks in your life.

If you say, "I am awful at locating what I need to work on in my own life." That's okay. Go to God and ask him to show you the leaks. He may reveal it to you in a dream. He may wake you up in the middle the night, just be sure to write it down so you can remember later on. He may even reveal it to you in prayer or through a song. He's going to be showing you something that needs to change, so don't take it as harsh correction. Take it as a hand from your father showing you the right way to go. He is still working on each of us, making us more like Him, but only if we allow Him to work on us.

"A small leak will sink a great ship."

-Benjamin Franklin

Day 89

Inner Voice

John 10:27, "My sheep listen to my voice; I know them, and they follow me."

The Bible says when you do not know how to pray, the Holy Spirit will lead you and guide you into all truth. God is with you every day increasing your knowledge and wisdom. When you ask, the Holy Spirit will give you the answer.

The Holy Spirit will even direct you in the small things like paying for the person behind you in the drive-through just to brighten their day. The little voice inside of you that says "bless them today". He could even remind you to pack something to take with you that you never would have thought to bring, but then you ended up really needing it.

We were on our way to church one morning, I felt that little voice saying, "Grab that beach towel". I looked twice at the towel on the counter thinking, "Why would I need that towel for church?" I grabbed the towel, not even realizing that it was the Holy Spirit preparing me for my future. All three children were loaded up in the car seats, my husband was driving and I was in the passenger seat. When we made our last left turn to pull into church, Michael said, "Mommy, I'm going to throw up!" Not even thinking, I put the towel on his lap just in time for him to throw up into that versus all over the back seat. I started crying. Not because I was mad about my son throwing up in our van, but because the Holy Spirit even prepared me for that "mommy moment". God is so good like that.

The Holy Spirit's voice will start out small, he wants to see if you'll learn to hear and be obedient. When you obey the Holy Spirit, He will begin to speak to you in a deeper way. He will show you how to become better at your job, help you to push yourself during a work-out, or even how to get that student loan paid off.

Allow yourself today to be sensitive to the Holy Spirit. He can lead you too and show you things that you never would be able to see before that you can accomplish when you listen to His voice.

"In order to hear God's voice, you must turn down the world's voice."

-Holly Taylor

Day 90

Your Child Needs You

Proverbs 22:6, "Start children off on the way they should go, and even when they are old they will not turn from it."

With God's guidance we can help our children come to know what their God-given calling is. First and foremost our children need to develop a relationship with Him just like it's important for us to build a relationship with Him. Our children need to know that God is there with them everywhere they go and that they can talk to Him about anything. They need to know that just going to church doesn't make them a Christian. It's talking with God and following His lead that causes our relationship with Jesus to grow. They need to know that even though sports are on Sundays, going to church can be more important. That might mean they miss out in playing a game scheduled during church, not because we are religious, but because we need our children to know that our relationship with Him comes first. Going to church helps our children come to know the big-little stories like Jonah and the big fish, Daniel in the lion's den, Queen Esther, and so many more. Those stories will stay with them for a lifetime and will encourage them in their walk of faith their whole life.

Yes, we as parents have a huge responsibility in helping our children establish a relationship with God. God will give you the grace to teach them exactly what they need to know. God will show you the right church for your family so other Christians can help pour into their lives. Parents, your children are watching you every day.

The church is supposed to be bigger than just a building. We can be the church all throughout the week. You can be the church through little acts of kindness like bringing dinner to a family who just came home from the hospital, or giving hand-me-downs to a family in need instead of selling them. It can be more than just a nice thing to do if it's something directed by God.

Is there something that you can do in your family's life that will help your children see you walking out your relationship with Christ every day other than just going to church on Sunday? Pray over them before they go to school in the morning, invite Jesus into your family's day-to-day life and I promise you, your children will see that being a Christian is so much more than going to church. It's walking in the ways Jesus wants us to go.

"If we don't teach our children to follow Christ, the world will teach them not to."

-Unknown Author

Day 91

God Your Shelter

Psalms 91:1, "Those who live in the shelter of the Most High will rest in the shadow of the Almighty."

God is with you wherever you go. Whatever you're facing, He is there with you. I remember when my husband left the first time to Iraq, we had been married for just 11 months. Everything was different around me. I was from a small town in Michigan and now I lived in a totally different environment in southern California. My husband left for Iraq on a Thursday in September of 2005. I, of course, was totally sad that day. Sunday came around and I went to church like normal, but something happened to me that service that had never happened before. During worship service I was just praising with my hands lifted high when all of a sudden I heard another voice right by me. I knew no one was sitting near me before worship service so I looked over. There he was, this angel. He was so tall, dressed in white and glowing. He was worshiping too. He looked over at me, put his hand on my shoulder and said, "Do not be afraid. God is with you". Then he was gone.

For a moment I was stunned and thought I was losing it since my husband just left. Then I begin to feel a peaceful presence surround me. The angel was sent just for me in that moment. Four days went by and I found out I was pregnant! I was so happy, but sad that I had no one was near to me to share the news with in person.

When we're reading scriptures and meditating on them, so much will happen for us. Things we wouldn't even think we needed will happen for our good. When I prayed Psalms 91 over Samuel and over myself, God was able to release the supernatural. I experienced great peace during his deployment. Sure I was still so sad, wanting to ball every time we would say good bye on the phone, but God was over me and He was with Samuel. Take hold of His peace today. Know God is with you.

On the next page there are places for you to make Psalms 91 personal to you. When I need reassurance of God's protection for either my spouse, our children or myself, I remind myself what it says by reading it. The word of God can bring so much peace, joy, healing and direction to our lives.

"Safety is not the absence of danger, but the presence of God."

–Jeanette Windle

Making Psalms 91 Personal

(I/loved one's name) will dwell in the shelter of the Most High. (I/loved one's name) will rest in the shadow of the Almighty. (I/loved one's name) will say of the Lord, "He is my refuge and my fortress, my God, in whom I trust." Surely He will save (Me/loved one's name) from the fowler's snare and from the deadly pestilence. He will cover (Me/loved one's name) with his feathers, and under his wings (I/loved one's name) will find refuge; his faithfulness will be (My/loved one's name) shield and rampart. (I/loved one's name) will not fear the terror of night, nor the arrow that flies by day, nor the pestilence that stalks in the darkness, nor the plague that destroys at midday. A thousand may fall at (My/loved one's name) side, ten thousand at your right hand, but it will not come near (Me/loved one's name). (I/loved one's name) will only observe with (My/His) eyes and see the punishment of the wicked. If (I/loved one's name) say, "The Lord is my refuge", no harm will overtake (Me/Him). No disaster will come near (My/Their) tent. For He will command His angels concerning (Me/loved one's name) to guard (Me/loved one's name) in all (My/Their) ways; they will lift (Me/loved one's name) up in their hands, so that (I/loved one's name) will not strike (My/His) foot against a stone. (I/loved one's name) will tread on the lion and the cobra; (I/loved one's name) will trample the great lion and the serpent. "Because (they) love me," says the Lord, "I will rescue (Her/Him); I will protect (Your name/loved one's name), for (She/He) acknowledges my name. (She/He) will call on me, and I will answer (them); I will be with (Your name/loved one's name) in trouble, I will deliver (Her/Him) and honor (Her/Him). With long life I will satisfy (Your name/loved one's name) and show (Her/Him) my salvation." Psalms 91

Special Thoughts

Dear Military Sister,

You are a prodigy (an impressive or outstanding example of a particular quality) of your Heavenly Father. Every day you desire and choose to follow after His ways you become more and more like Him. Others will look to you for help because they see that you are different. They see you getting an extra dose of strength and they know you are a true follower of Jesus. You are a prodigy of Jesus.

As you finish this devotional book, know you are at the right place at the right time. There is no question why you are where you are. You were made for more than to just be hanging out on your couch, getting sucked into a TV series, or to just go with the flow. Always know God is with you no matter where the military sends you. The military may say they just need to fill a spot but the truth is that God opened that spot just for you and your family.

Never doubt what God has told you to do. Remember if God planted the seed in you, He will be with you every step of the way until you see that dream fulfilled.

Be on guard always. Your husband trains for war for weeks, even months before going. Likewise, you also need to train for the unseen spiritual war every day!

Let me pray with you:

Dear God, I pray the power of the Holy Spirit will arise in my friend, that you make her way straight and bring clarity amongst the chaos the military can bring. When the world says she should be stressing, release your peace that only you can bring, for it is in you we find peace!

Thank you for her sweet and confident spirit she has during a chaotic military schedule. Thank you for giving her wisdom beyond her years, bless her Lord, bless her family, her husband and their place of living.

I pray you will open the doors that need to be opened and close the doors that need to be closed. I ask you, Lord, to protect her and the calling you have on her life. Jesus, I pray you give her boldness to stand out for you. I thank you for giving her the right words at the right time. Thank you for her, thank you for helping her advance in the calling you have on her life. Help her, Jesus, to be the best military spouse there is. Give her a compassionate heart for the other military and non-military spouses around her. I thank you for her, Lord. Thank you Jesus for your love! In Jesus' name, Amen.

You know what you must do, now do it. Walk the word out! Put the word to work in every area of your life. You got this, Sista!

Hugs Tight,

Katherine Monit

Luke 1:45, "Blessed is she who has believed that the Lord would fulfill his promises to her!"

Military Terms Used Throughout the Devotional

PCS- Permanente change of duty station

PFT- Physical fitness test

Monitor- Service member of other given the role of planning the future assignments for a pacific occupation specialty.

MEU- Marine expeditionary unit. Comprised of multiply units from various occupational specialties joining together to form one unit capable of delivery of lethal force within relatively a short time frame. Some military spouses call the MEU the boat.

Marine Corps Ball- Marine birthday celebration

Field Day- Nickname referring to a deep clean.

Drill Team- Group of either handpicked or volunteer service members who perform traditional drill movements in a predetermined event.

Taped In- Method by which a members body fat percentage is determined. This is used when a service member exceeds allowable weight limit for height and age.

Duty Station- A place where the service members works.

BAH- Basic Housing Allowance.

MCX- Marine Corps. Exchange.

Squadron- Equivalent of company sized unit from 250-400 members, depending on the aircraft assigned to the specific aviation unit.

Package- An application process involving filling out multiple documents and undergoing physical examination which validate an individual is fit physically and experience wise for the position to which they are applying for.

*The definitions given here are from personal experience of Samuel Monit.

Write Your Vision

Habakkuk 2:2, "And the LORD answered me: "Write the vision; make it plain on tablets, so he may run who reads it."

Write (or if you're an artist, draw) your vison clearly, things that you have wanted to do for years. Maybe it's to just clean out your closets, keep the car clean for three days straight, anything you have been wanting to make a priority in your own life. When you have a list of your vision you can see them and gain motivation!

Made in the USA
Middletown, DE
15 October 2023

40872971R00136